INTERNATIONAL RELATIONS 1919-39

Keith Shepha...

GENERAL EDITOR Jon Nichol

Contents

Basil Blackwell

Introduction

A Wounded French soldiers leaving the battlefield near Rheims, 1914

This book begins and ends with photographs showing the suffering caused by war. The first photograph (**A**) shows some of the soldiers wounded in the First World War, in which 20 million people died. The last photograph (**B** on page 48) was taken in 1940, early in the Second World War, in which another 37 million people were to die.

The 20 or so years that passed between these two photographs were taken up with international attempts to establish a lasting peace in Europe. At the end of the First World War a League of Nations was set up; such an organisation, it was hoped, would enable nations to sort out their disputes by negotiation rather than war. The League relied on the idea of *collective security* to preserve peace in Europe. But as early as 1923 the League showed it was not strong enough to keep the Great Powers (the major nations in Europe) in check. **B** shows the changing pattern of events 1919–39. The outbreak of the Second World War in 1939 proved how unsuccessful these attempts to secure peace were. But why did they fail?

This book shows the pattern of international events that led to a second world war just 20 years after the first. Pages 3–7 look at how the statesmen tried to sort out Europe in 1919–20, and how the peace treaties they drew up were challenged. Pages 8–13 show how France, Germany and Russia approached international relations in the 1920s. The work of the League of Nations in the 1920s is examined on pages 14–17.

In 1929 the world was hit by a trade slump and depression. Pages 18–20 look at its international causes and effects. A case study then investigates the rise of Mediterranean Fascism (page 21) in Portugal (page 22), Italy (pages 23–29) and Spain, where it resulted in Civil War (pages 30–33).

In the 1930s Japanese aggression led to the breakdown of international relations in the Far East (see pages 34–37). By the mid-1930s it was clear that the League of Nations had failed (pages 38–39). Pages 40–47 examine the steps that led to the outbreak of war in Europe, and page 48 outlines how America became involved.

B Europe 1919–39

1919–20 A number of peace treaties were drawn up at the end of the First World War. These treaties had serious flaws, and the terms were bitterly resented by the 'losing' countries in the war. But attempts to establish a lasting peace continued.

1930s In the early and mid-1930s a world economic depression made international cooperation more difficult. There was mass unemployment and poverty, which helped Hitler and the Nazis to power in Germany. Attempts to guarantee peace and promote disarmament were frustrated.

In the late 1930s insecurity, fear and aggression led countries to protect themselves with alliances and build up stocks of arms.

?????????????????

Look closely at the picture on the front cover of this book. It shows Republican fighters in the Spanish Civil War.
a What clues does the photograph give us about the Republican Army? (Think about: uniform; weapons; age and sex of the fighters . . .)
b What do you think might have happened shortly before this photograph was taken?
c Imagine you are one of the people in the photograph. How do you feel about the cause you are fighting for? What image of yourself/the Republicans, do you want the photograph to give?
d How useful are such photographs to the historian? What problems might there be in using photographs as historical evidence?

1 Suffering and peace

After more than four years of fighting, the First World War ended on 11 November 1918. Philip Gibbs, a journalist, reported from France:

❝Last night, for the first time since August in the first year of the war, there was no light of gunfire in the sky, no sudden stabs of flame through darkness, no spreading glow above black trees where for four years of nights human beings were smashed to death. The Fires of Hell had been put out.❞ (A)   The New York Times

Where the fighting had been fiercest, in north-eastern France and parts of Belgium, Russia, Austria and Bulgaria, farms, roads, factories, railways and towns were wrecked (**B**). **C** lists the damage suffered by both sides.

The victors – Britain, France and the USA – believed that someone had to take the blame for the war and pay for the damage. They were also determined to make sure that such destruction would never happen again. In January 1919 the 'Big Three' leaders, Lloyd George (Prime Minister of Britain), Clemenceau (Prime Minister of France) and Wilson (President of the USA), met, together with the Italian leader, Orlando, at Versailles, near Paris. There they decided on the terms of the peace treaties the defeated countries would have to sign.

Most people in Britain, France and the USA were bitter and angry at all they had suffered. They blamed Germany for starting the war, and demanded that the Germans pay *reparations* (compensation) for the damage. Many wanted to deal Germany such a severe blow that it could never recover to fight again.

D shows the points the Allies had to consider at the Versailles talks.

Allies	Soldiers killed	Other damage
France	1 400 000	North-east France ruined by fighting
Britain	750 000	Spent nine billion pounds on the war (some of which was borrowed money)
Belgium	50 000	Suffered great damage from fighting and German occupation
Italy	600 000	North-east Italy devastated by fighting
USA	116 000	Entered the war late in 1917 and suffered least
Russia	1 700 000	The war led to revolution, a communist takeover and the loss of much land
Central powers		
Germany	2 000 000	Little damage but revolution and hunger at the end of the war
Austria–Hungary	1 200 000	
Turkey	375 000	
Bulgaria	100 000	
TOTAL Approximately 20 000 000 soldiers and civilians died due to the war		

C Aftermath of the First World War

D Issues discussed at Versailles

1 Should they put Kaiser Wilhelm (the ruler of Germany) on trial for starting the war?
2 Who was guilty of starting the war?
3 Should Germany be forced to pay reparations? If so, how much?
4 Should Germany be allowed to keep any armed forces at all? If so, how many?
5 Should Germany be allowed to have any colonies? If not, should they become independent? Or should they come under the control of a new international organisation – the League of Nations?
6 What about the German-speaking people in Austria? Some Austrians might want to unite with Germany – should this be allowed?
7 What should happen to territory on the borders of Germany which both the Germans and neighbouring countries claimed (see map **E**)?

B The ruins of Ypres, at the centre of some of the fiercest fighting in the First World War.

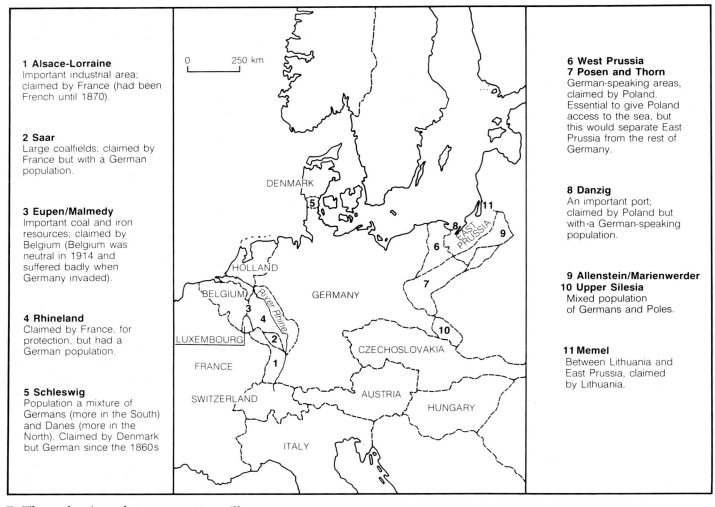

1 Alsace-Lorraine
Important industrial area;
claimed by France (had been
French until 1870).

2 Saar
Large coalfields; claimed by
France but with a German
population.

3 Eupen/Malmedy
Important coal and iron
resources; claimed by
Belgium (Belgium was
neutral in 1914 and
suffered badly when
Germany invaded).

4 Rhineland
Claimed by France, for
protection, but had a
German population.

5 Schleswig
Population a mixture of
Germans (more in the South)
and Danes (more in the
North). Claimed by Denmark
but German since the 1860s

6 West Prussia
7 Posen and Thorn
German-speaking areas,
claimed by Poland.
Essential to give Poland
access to the sea, but
this would separate East
Prussia from the rest of
Germany.

8 Danzig
An important port;
claimed by Poland but
with a German-speaking
population.

9 Allenstein/Marienwerder
10 Upper Silesia
Mixed population
of Germans and Poles.

11 Memel
Between Lithuania and
East Prussia, claimed
by Lithuania.

E The reshaping of Europe at Versailles

F President Wilson's '14 Points'

Aim: to prevent another war
1 No more secret treaties between countries
2 The seas to be free to ships of all nations
3 No restrictions on trade between countries
4 All countries to reduce armaments
5 The wishes of people in colonies to be considered when
other countries claimed those colonies

Aim: to achieve self-determination (the right of each person
to live in their own country)
6 Russia to be free to choose its own system of government
7 Belgium to be independent
8 Alsace-Lorraine to be returned to France
9 Italy's frontiers to be redrawn along lines of nationality
10 Different nationalities in the Austro–Hungarian Empire to
be allowed self-government
11 People in the Balkans to be free to form their own
countries
12 Non-Turkish people in the Turkish Empire to be free to
form their own countries
13 Poland to be independent
14 An international organisation to be set up to protect the
independence of countries and settle disputes

Treaties and terms

President Wilson arrived at the Versailles talks with '14
points' which he was sure would create a lasting peace. F
outlines these points, and what they aimed to achieve.

Lloyd George, the British Prime Minister, agreed with
many of Wilson's 14 points. He could see that a harsh
treaty might lead to more trouble in the future. But the
British public demanded that Lloyd George should take a
tough line with Germany.

Clemenceau, the French leader (nicknamed 'The Tiger')
wanted to punish Germany and make the Germans too
weak ever to attack France again.

It took several months of talks before the leaders finally
reached a decision. G shows the terms of the treaties they
drew up with Germany, Austria, Hungary and Bulgaria.
(The Treaty of Sèvres, with Turkey, is described on page
6).

The new Europe

By the end of 1919 the new shape of Europe was emerging (see map inside front cover). Before the First World War there had been five great powers in Europe, like five boxers in one ring. But Austria–Hungary had collapsed; Russia was out of the ring for the time being, occupied with civil war at home; Germany had been knocked down, and its hands were tied by the terms of the Treaty of Versailles. On the fringes of Europe, the Turkish Empire had also collapsed. Of the former great powers, only Britain and France were left – both exhausted, but still on their feet.

There were also the new, independent countries, such as Poland, Czechoslovakia, Yugoslavia and the Baltic States of Lithuania, Estonia and Finland. Some of these were weak and poor; it was clear they would be no match for Germany or Russia should either recover its strength. Moreover, in some of the new countries there were people from different national groups; many of them wanted to be independent, or to belong to some other country. Three million German-speaking people lived in what was now the Sudeten area of Czechoslovakia; there were Hungarians in Rumania and Czechoslovakia, and Germans in Poland (see E). These 'problem' areas might well threaten the peace of Europe if neighbouring countries could not settle their disputes.

Much of Europe was in chaos. Millions of people were unemployed; returning soldiers could not find work, and others lost their jobs when factories stopped making weapons. Industry and trade were in decline. In some countries, money lost its value, so buying and selling was difficult. Most goods were moved by rail, but much of the European railway system was in ruins. Production of vital supplies such as grain and coal was low, and people were already starving in Germany and Austria. Then, in 1919, an influenza virus hit Europe. Hungry people have little resistance to germs, and the 'Spanish flu' spread rapidly. 27 million people died in the epidemic.

These were just some of the problems that faced those who were trying to rebuild a peaceful, prosperous Europe.

G The peace treaties

Treaty of Versailles with Germany, 28 June 1919
1 The Kaiser to be put on trial (this never happened – he had fled to safety in Holland)
2 Germany was declared guilty of starting the war
3 Germany to pay reparations for war damages (later fixed at £6 600 000 000)
4 Germany allowed an army of 100 000 men and a small navy, but no tanks, warplanes or submarines
5 German colonies to be put under the control of the League of Nations
6 Union with Austria (Anschluss) forbidden
7 New frontiers drawn up (see map **E**):
  ● Alsace–Lorraine (**1**) to France
  ● the Saar (**2**) to come under League of Nations control for 15 years, then to have a plebiscite (vote) to decide its future
  ● Eupen/Malmedy (**3**) to Belgium
  ● the Rhineland (**4**) to be kept by Germany, but demilitarised (ie no troops or fortifications)
  ● Schleswig (**5**) – after a plebiscite, the North to Denmark, the South to Germany
  ● West Prussia, Posen and Thorn (**6**, **7**) to Poland
  ● Danzig (**8**) to be a 'Free City' controlled by the League of Nations
  ● Allenstein/Marienwerder (**9**) – after plebiscites, kept by Germany
  ● Upper Silesia (**10**) – after plebiscite, Western half kept by Germany, Eastern half to Poland
  ● Memel (**11**) under League of Nations control
8 A League of Nations to be set up
As a result of the Treaty of Versailles, Germany lost 13% of its area, 12% of population, 16% of coal resources and 48% of iron production

Treaty of St Germain with Austria, Sept 1919
Treaty of Trianon with Hungary, June 1920
1 Austria and Hungary to be small, separate states
2 Territory lost:
  ● Bohemia, Moravia, Slovakia to the new Czechoslovakia
  ● South Tyrol, Istria, Trieste to Italy
  ● Dalmatia, Bosnia, Croatia to the new Yugoslavia
  ● Galicia to Poland
  ● Transylvania to Rumania
3 Austria and Hungary to pay reparations and reduce armaments

Treaty of Neuilly with Bulgaria, Nov 1919
1 Western Thrace to Greece, other land to Yugoslavia
2 Bulgaria to pay reparations and reduce armaments

??????????????????

1 Study **F** and **G**.
  a Which of Wilson's 14 points were included in the peace treaties?
  b Which terms in the peace treaties were *not* in Wilson's 14 points?

2 In groups of 3, each of you take on the role of one of the Big Three leaders at Versailles. For each of the points in **D**, act out how the talks might have gone. What standpoint would you have taken? What arguments would you have put forward to support that view? Would you have managed to agree? Reached a compromise? Disagreed?

3 Write a brief newspaper report headed 'Europe 1919: Problems'. Base your report on the following paragraph openings, and place them in what you think is their order of importance:
There is hunger and starvation . . ., Many Germans now live outside Germany . . .; Unemployment is . . .; Spanish influenza . . .; Europe's railways . . .

2 Challenges to the peace treaties

Many Germans were angry about the peace treaties. They believed they had been treated unfairly. The German Economic Commission warned:

In a very short time Germany will not be in a position to give bread and work to her numerous millions of inhabitants ... Those who sign this Treaty will sign the death of many millions of German men, women and children. **(A)**

It was not only the Germans who criticised the treaties (**B**). One of the main objections was over the payment of *reparations* (compensation). In 1920 the British economist John Maynard Keynes warned that the treaties would prevent the European economy recovering from the damage the war had done:

The Treaties include nothing to make the defeated Central Empires (Germany and Austria) into good neighbours, nothing to stabilise the new States of Europe, nothing to reclaim Russia ... no arrangement for restoring the disordered finances of France and Italy ... The danger facing us, therefore, is the drop of the standard of life of the European population to a point which will mean actual starvation for some. **(C)**

B Opposition to the peace treaties

Germany was angry over three main issues:
1 loss of territory and people. The city of Danzig and the surrounding area, where two million Germans lived, was made a 'Free City' to form part of the 'Polish corridor' linking Poland to the sea. Three million Germans lived in the Sudetenland, which now became part of Czechoslovakia.
2 all the blame for causing the war was placed on Germany.
3 reparations – in 1921 Germany was ordered to pay £6 600 000 000 although it had no way of raising money.

France – many thought that Germany had been let off too lightly; they were afraid that there were not enough safeguards to prevent Germany attacking again.

Italy felt cheated at not receiving Dalmatia, which was given to Yugoslavia.

Hungary – many people in Transylvania (Magyars) were Hungarian, but it was given to Romania.

Poland and Czechoslovakia both laid claim to Teschen and did not like having to split it between them.

Turkey Mustapha Kemal mounted a successful challenge to the Treaty of Sèvres and won back much of the territory Turkey had lost.

Ten years later Sir Philip Gibbs, a British journalist, claimed:

It was a peace of vengeance. It reeked with injustice. It was incapable of fulfilment. It sowed a thousand seeds from which new wars might spring ... The absurdity, the wild impossibility, of extracting that vast tribute (reparations) from the defeated enemy ... ought to have been obvious to the most ignorant schoolboy ... **(D)**

One of the aims of the peacemakers had been to set up a system of self-determination – that is, to allow national groups to form their own country and government. But this rarely worked in practice. It was impossible to draw clear boundaries between different national groups, who might live in different countries, or mixed with other peoples. The re-drawing of boundaries might also mean that some countries were weak and did not have the natural defences, resources or industry necessary to protect themselves against other, stronger nations.

Think about the people listed below, living in Europe in 1919. How would each of them feel about the treaties? Would he or she be angry? Frightened? What hopes or fears might they have about the future?

German factory worker (female) living in the port of Danzig. This had been part of Germany but in 1919 it was made a 'Free city' under the control of the League of Nations.

German teacher (female) in the Sudetenland. This was a German-speaking area, part of the old Austro–Hungarian Empire. In 1919 it become part of Czechoslovakia.

Hungarian soldier who had fought against Romania in the war. He lived in Transylvania, in eastern Hungary, which became part of Romania in 1919.

Polish coalminer living in the city of Teschen and working in nearby coalmines. Both Czechoslovakia and Poland had good reason to claim the area. The Allies bullied both countries into accepting an agreement whereby Poland kept Teschen and Czechoslovakia got the coalmines and the railway station.

French lawyer born in Alsace-Lorraine. In 1871 Prussia (Germany) had taken this area from France. In 1919 it was given back to France.

Corporal in the German army who had been born in Austria and fought for Germany in the war. He dreamed of the day when Germany would become great again and recover the land it had lost.

Young Turkish army officer who had fought against the Allies (including Turkey's bitter enemy, Greece) during the war. In 1920 the Treaty of Sèvres gave Greece control of parts of Turkey. There were British, French and Italian troops in other parts of the country.

The French lawyer, Poincaré, was President of France and later became Prime Minister. The Corporal in the German army was Adolf Hitler. His dream of a new, powerful Germany came true in the 1930s (see pages 10–11). The only one of these people to challenge the treaties immediately and fulfil his hopes quickly was the young Turkish officer, Mustapha Kemal (**E**).

The ruler of Turkey was the Sultan, but by 1919 he did what the Allies told him. In 1920 he agreed to the conditions of the Treaty of Sèvres. Turkey lost Eastern Thrace and Smyrna to Greece (see map **F**), had to give up control of the Straits into the Black Sea to an International Commission, and lost colonies in Syria and Palestine. Many Turks were angered by this, and refused to accept the Sultan's rule. In 1920 Mustapha Kemal set up a rival government in Ankara. He warned his followers:

❝ *The Sultan and his government are prisoners in the hands of the Allies. We are about to lose our country. I have come to seek your help and save the situation ... We are fighting with our backs to the wall, but we will fight to the end. We demand the right of every sovereign (independent) state to be free within our own boundaries. We ask nothing more and nothing less.* ❞ (**G**)

In Britain *The Times* newspaper described Kemal and his nationalist supporters as 'a minority of adventurers, criminals and fanatics'. But *The Times* was wrong. In

E Mustapha Kemal (centre). When he came to power, Kemal took the name 'Ataturk' – Father of the Turks

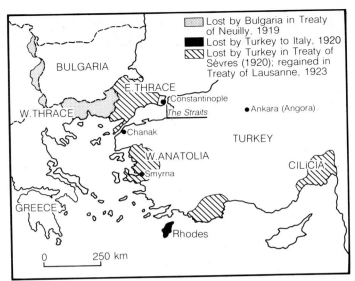

Lost by Bulgaria in Treaty of Neuilly, 1919
Lost by Turkey to Italy, 1920
Lost by Turkey in Treaty of Sèvres (1920); regained in Treaty of Lausanne, 1923

F Turkey and the peace treaties

1921 a Greek army threatened Kemal's stronghold at Ankara. In the Battle of Inönü which followed, Kemal and his supporters destroyed the Greek forces. The next year, 1922, he defeated the Greeks at Smyrna. The occupying French and Italian troops withdrew from Turkey, leaving only the British forces stationed at Chanak – blocking the road to Constantinople, Turkey's capital.

Most British people were against fighting the Turks. The British agreed to discuss a new peace treaty. Turkey was no longer a defeated enemy. Instead, the country was seen as a victor which had won its independence. A new treaty was signed at Lausanne in Switzerland in 1923. Turkey got back Eastern Thrace and Smyrna and regained control of the Straits. Over one million Greeks living in Turkey were forced to leave their homes, and about 400000 Turks left Greece.

??????????????

1 a On which point does **C** agree with **A**?
  b What great danger does **D** warn about?
  c If **A** was the only evidence of criticism of the peace treaties, why might a historian doubt it?
  d How do **C** and **D** help the historian be more confident about criticism of the peace treaties? Why?

2 a What impression does **E** give of Mustapha Kemal?
  b In **G**, how does Kemal justify his fight to overthrow the Sultan?
  c How effective do you think **G** would be in winning him support? (Think about: use of language, appeal to the emotions . . .)

3 Write an essay to explain 'Who criticised the peace treaties and why?'

3 The French search for security

1 358 000 soldiers killed
2 500 000 soldiers wounded
23 000 factories destroyed
5600 km of railway line wrecked
2 000 000 people forced to flee from their homes
300 000 houses destroyed
90% of coal and iron industry destroyed
£5 392 000 000 spent on defence (A)

Look at **A**. How would you feel if so much destruction happened in your country? This was what happened to France in the First World War. Most of the fighting took place in France, so it suffered more than any other country. At the end of the war the French people wanted revenge, compensation and a guarantee that Germany would never invade their country again (**B**).

When he met the other Allied leaders at Versailles the French Prime Minister, George Clemenceau, tried to make sure that the Treaty would make Germany pay for the war and leave the Germans too weak to attack again. However, the Treaty of Versailles did not really solve the problem. Germany was still a threat, as the modern historian A J P Taylor explains:

❛ . . . Germany remained by far the greatest Power on the continent of Europe . . . (it) was greatest in population – 65 million against 40 million in France, the only other major Power. German superiority was greater still in the economic resources of coal and steel which in modern times

B In this satirical poster the French leader is forcing a defeated Germany to drink disinfectant

D The strength of France and Germany in 1914 and 1938–9

	1914		1938–9	
	France	*Germany*	*France*	*Germany*
Population	39 601 509	65 000 000	41 600 000	68 424 000
Troops	3 500 000	8 500 000	800 000	800 000
Reserve troops			4 600 000	2 200 000
Aircraft			600	4 500
Steel production (tons)	4 333 000	17 024 000	6 200 000	20 500 000
Coal production (tons)	40 800 000	279 000 000	46 500 000	169 200 000

together made up power . . . nothing could prevent the Germans from overshadowing Europe, even if they did not plan to do so. ❜ (**C**)

(*The Origins of the Second World War,* 1969)

Chart **D** compares the strength of France and Germany between 1914 and 1939.

The French remembered the German invasions of 1871 and 1914. They feared the Germans might try again. Unlike Britain or the USA, France was open to attack from the East, as Clemenceau explained:

❛I beg you to understand my state of mind . . . America is far away and protected by the ocean. England could not be reached easily. You are sheltered, both of you, we are not . . . We need a barrier behind which, in the years to come, our people can work in security to rebuild the ruins. That barrier is the river Rhine.❜ (**E**)

France wanted control of the Rhine and its bridges. But the other Allies would not agree to this, since it would mean more than five million Germans coming under French control. Instead, Germany had to accept that Allied troops were to occupy the area west of the Rhine for 15 years, and that a 50-mile strip east of the Rhine would be *demilitarised* (no German troops or fortresses would be allowed there).

Many French people were disappointed in the Treaty of Versailles. Andre Maginot, a French politician, warned:

❛We are always the invaded, we are always the ones to suffer. Fifteen invasions in less than six centuries give us the right to insist upon a victor's treaty that will offer something more realistic than temporary solutions and uncertain hopes . . .❜ (**F**)

The USA refused to *ratify* (confirm) the Treaty. Britain would not guarantee help against Germany. France did not feel that it could rely on the League of Nations for protection. So the French leaders looked for other ways of obtaining security. During the 1920s France kept a large army, and formed alliances with Germany's other neighbours: Belgium (1920); Poland (1921); Czechoslovakia (1924); Romania (1926) and Yugoslavia (1927). Under these agreements, the nations promised to keep to the frontiers set down in 1919–20.

But there was another problem. How could France make Germany pay reparations for all the war damage? The Germans claimed they did not have the money, but the French Prime Minister, Poincaré, believed this was just an excuse. In January 1923 he sent French soldiers to occupy the Ruhr area of Germany (**G**). Belgium also sent troops. The Ruhr was the industrial heart of Germany, producing three quarters of the country's coal and steel. Poincaré was determined to take what Germany owed to France:

❝*We are going to look for coal, that's all! . . . We have no intention of strangling Germany or ruining her, we only want to obtain from her what we can reasonably expect her to provide.* ❞ (**H**)

It was not that easy. The Germans were bitterly resentful. German workers in the Ruhr went on strike and

G French soldiers guarding the Reichsbank in Essen, Germany, January 1923

adopted a policy of *passive resistance*. This meant that they would not cooperate with the French. One German remembered:

❝*Wherever foreign soldiers appeared, German workers downed tools. The trains stopped running, the steelworks and factories emptied, the miners went home, farmers hid their food stocks, many shopkeepers locked up their premises . . . life came to a standstill.* ❞ (**J**)

(Egon Larsen *Weimar Eyewitness*, 1976)

The French brought in their own workers, but this did not solve the problem. They even tried to persuade the people in the Rhineland to set up a separate state, but the attempt failed.

The occupation of the Ruhr put a tremendous strain on the Germany economy. Before long, it cracked. The value of the mark (German currency) fell until it was almost worthless (see pages 10–11). The occupation also caused trouble and expense in France. In 1924 Poincaré fell from power. He returned in 1926, but under the new government French foreign policy was controlled by Aristide Briand. Briand tried to improve relations with Germany and protect France by making alliances and working through the League of Nations.

In 1925 Germany and the other European powers met at Locarno in Switzerland in a further attempt to secure peace. But French fear of Germany ran deep. Between 1930 and 1935 France built a massive line of fortresses – the Maginot Line – along the border with Germany.

??????????????????

1 a According to A J P Taylor (**C**) why did Germany remain a threat after the First World War?
b Why did Clemenceau think that control of the Rhine was so important (**E**)?
c What did Maginot mean by 'a victor's treaty' (**F**)?
d What is meant by 'passive resistance'?

2 a What does **B** tell us about French feelings towards Germany?
b What impression of Germany is the advertisement trying to give?

3 Look at **D**
a What do the figures show about Germany's industrial strength compared with that of France?
b What do the figures for 1938–9 suggest about what France believed to be important for defence?
c Why are the steel, coal and manufacturing figures important?

4 Use the evidence in this section and on the back cover to write an essay entitled 'Why and how did France search for security after the war?'

4 Germany and the world 1919–33

After the war Germany faced many problems. Opposition groups attempted to overthrow the Government in 1919, 1920 and 1923 (see **A** and *Germany* in this series). Germany was an outcast in Europe, excluded from the League of Nations. The surrounding countries – France, Belgium, Poland and Czechoslovakia – distrusted Germany. They had gained territory from Germany in 1919 and did not want the Germans to recover their military strength. In May 1921 a huge reparations bill of £6 600 000 000 was presented to Germany (**B**).

Germany turned to the other outcast in Europe, Communist Russia, as a possible ally. In 1921 they made secret business agreements which allowed German firms to make aeroplanes, submarines and weapons in Russia (the Treaty of Versailles had banned Germany from possessing such weapons). In April 1922 the two countries signed the Treaty of Rapallo, under which they agreed to resume 'normal relations' and cancel outstanding debts.

In 1923 France sent soldiers into Germany to occupy the Ruhr (see page 9). The occupation dealt a serious blow to the German economy, which collapsed under the

B Germany 'Ach! Aindt it too far?'
Answer 'The first seven million miles are the hardest, after that you get used to it.'

A Germany 1919–34

1919	*Jan* Spartacist (Communist) rising fails
	Feb Weimar Republic formed. Treaty of Versailles
1920	Kapp Putsch – a right-wing attempt to overthrow Government – fails. National Socialist German Workers Party (Nazi Party) formed
1921	Reparations set at £6 600 000 000
1922	Treaty of Rapallo with Russia
1923	*Jan* Ruhr occupied by French and Belgian troops
	Aug Stresemann becomes Chancellor
	Rapid inflation
	Nov Hitler's Munich Putsch fails
1924	Dawes Plan begins
1925	Locarno Treaties
1926	Germany joins League of Nations
1928	13 Nazi deputies elected to Reichstag
1929	Young Plan begins. Stresemann dies
1930	107 Nazi deputies elected
1931	Unemployment reaches 4 300 000
1932	230 Nazi deputies elected. Unemployment reaches 6 000 000
1933	*Jan* Hitler becomes Chancellor
	Feb Reichstag Fire
	Mar 288 Nazi deputies elected
	Jul Other political parties banned
	Oct Germany withdraws from League of Nations
1934	Hitler becomes Führer

strain. Prices rose sharply and the value of the German mark fell rapidly. As food prices rose, many people faced starvation. By November 1923 a single match cost 900 000 marks and a bottle of beer cost 150 000 000 000 marks (see **C**). A German journalist later wrote:

❝*Bartering became more and more widespread. A haircut cost a couple of eggs, and craftsmen such as watchmakers displayed notices: "Repairs carried out in exchange for food" . . . You went into a cafe and ordered a cup of coffee at the price shown, an hour later, when you asked for the bill, it had gone up by half or even double . . .*❞ (**D**)

(Egon Larsen *Weimar Eyewitness*, 1976)

In August 1923 Gustav Stresemann became Chancellor. Then, in November, he was made Foreign Minister. Stresemann realised that Germany had to cooperate with its former enemies, and he ended passive resistance in the Ruhr. Meanwhile, an international committee met to examine Germany's economic problems, headed by an American, Charles Dawes. In 1924 it recommended that:

- reparations should be paid at a reduced rate;
- the Germany currency should be reorganised;
- an international loan should be raised to help Germany.

Stresemann accepted the Dawes Plan and American loans poured into Germany, enabling it to pay some of the reparations bill and restart industries. However, this was an artificial way of paying debts – the American money was simply going round in circles.

In 1925 Britain, France, Italy, Belgium and Germany met as equals in Locarno in Switzerland, and signed

C As inflation soared even everyday items cost fantastic amounts of money. Shopkeepers had to use baskets or teachests to hold their takings

Then, in October 1929, Stresemann died. His death coincided with the start of a world economic crisis, sparked off by the Wall Street Crash in America (see *Modern America* in this series). The Depression hit Germany hard. All reparation payments were suspended and the Young Plan was forgotten. The good work of Stresemann was undone, unemployment rose rapidly and many people went hungry.

Such conditions gave the Nazi Party, and its leader Adolf Hitler, the chance to seize power. Nazi ideas, and those of other extreme political parties, offered hope to many unemployed people, helping them to forget their problems. Egon Larsen explains:

❛*The life of a young jobless worker was often intolerable. On dole days he had to join an endless queue outside his labour exchange* (job centre) *waiting for hours for his turn . . . those political organisations* (Nazis and Communists) *offered him some kind of social life at the end of the day, a uniform which made him feel important, and perhaps a plate of soup or a sandwich. The evening usually began with a get-together and a pep talk by some propaganda officer at the local headquarters – the backroom of a pub – and the men went on a "patrol" of the district, looking for trouble.*❜ **(G)**

E The Locarno Treaties

1 Germany, France and Belgium agreed that their borders were final (fixed). Britain and Italy guaranteed this.
2 The Rhineland to remain demilitarised.
3 France promised to protect Poland and Czechoslovakia if they were attacked by Germany.
4 Germany agreed not to use force to change its borders with Poland and Czechoslovakia.

several treaties intended to make Europe a safer place. E shows the most important agreements.

In 1926 Germany joined the League of Nations. One French journalist remembered:

❛*I was drunk with joy. It seemed too good to be true that Germany, our enemy of yesterday, had actually signed the pact. From now on, no more fears for the future! No more war! I was not alone in my blind enthusiasm. Everyone in Locarno was jubilant.*❜ **(F)**

In fact Locarno did little more than repeat the Treaty of Versailles. It left Russia feeling even more insecure (see pages 12–13). Most of the agreements were to be broken in the 1930s.

By 1929 all looked well for the Weimar Republic in Germany. Prosperity had returned. When the Dawes Plan ended in 1929 a new plan, the Young Plan, was arranged to deal with reparations. It reduced reparations by three quarters and gave Germany until 1988 to pay them off.

??????????????????

1 Look at **B**
  a What is keeping Germany going and what is dragging it back?
  b How does the cartoonist show his disapproval of reparations?

2 a What does photograph **C** tell us about Germany in the 1920s?
  b How useful are such pictures to the historian?

3 According to Egon Larsen in **G**, why did so many unemployed people join extreme political parties?

4 a Why were many people 'jubilant' when Germany joined the League of Nations (**F**)?
  b Many countries, including Germany, broke the Locarno agreements, so the predictions made in **F** were wrong. Does this make the account useless as historical evidence? Give reasons for your answer.

5 a Make brief notes on the following: Dawes Plan; Young Plan; reparations; passive resistance; Gustav Stresemann.
  b For each, explain its importance: for Germany; for Europe.

6 In pairs, as if you were French government advisers, draw up a plan of action to follow in your relations with Germany after 1929.

5 Russia and the world 1919–34

What do you fear or hate most? Snakes? School? You probably would not say 'ideas', yet many people fear or hate other people's ideas and beliefs. Winston Churchill, a member of the British Government in 1919, feared Communist ideas and beliefs more than anything.

❛*Communism is not a policy, it is a disease. Communism means war of the most ruthless character, the slaughter of men, women, and children, the burning of homes, and the inviting in of tyranny, disease, and famine . . .*❜ (A)

Many people in capitalist countries such as the USA and Britain fear and hate communist ideas; for their part, communist countries fear and hate capitalist ideas. Communists believe that all factories, mines, banks and other means of producing wealth should be owned and controlled by the State, whereas capitalists believe such things should be owned by individuals.

In 1917 there was a Communist Revolution in Russia. Before the Revolution Russia had been fighting against Germany in the First World War. To enable the Revolution to succeed the new Russian leader, Lenin, made peace with Germany. This angered Russia's former allies, Britain, France, the USA and Japan. They sent troops to fight the Communists in the civil war which followed the Revolution in Russia (B). By 1919 these forces had been defeated and all except the Japanese had withdrawn.

In the 1920s and early '30s capitalist countries gradually came to accept Russia. It was not easy – Lenin believed that it was his duty to encourage communist revolutions in other countries. Karl Marx (the founder of Communism) had written:

❛*Let the ruling classes tremble at a Communist revolution. In it the proletarians* (workers) *have nothing to lose but their chains. They have a world to win. Working men of all countries unite!*❜ (C)

Communist risings took place in Germany, Austria and Hungary but they were badly organised and easily crushed. In 1919 Lenin set up the Communist International (usually known as the Comintern) to help spread communist ideas and plan revolutions. It soon became clear, however, that Russia was not strong enough to bring about world communist revolution. This was demonstrated in 1920 when Poland attacked Russia. In March 1921 Russia had to agree to the Treaty of Riga, in which it lost territory to Poland.

Revolution and civil war had left Russia in ruins. A long drought caused a severe famine in 1921, in which over one million people died (D). Some countries, especially the USA, sent help in the form of food, medicine and clothing. Fridtjof Nansen, a Norwegian, headed a huge Red Cross project which sent 80000 tons of food to starving Russians.

The Russian leaders realised they would have to come

B Russian prisoners of war in an allied prison camp in Russia

D Russian famine victims, October 1921

to terms with the major capitalist powers. They tried to persuade other countries to officially recognise the communist government and to trade with Russia. In April 1922 Russia signed the Treaty of Rapallo with Germany (see page 11). This brought German money and experts to Russia.

Between 1922 and 1932 relations with other countries improved, but Russia remained suspicious of the capitalist powers. The Russians believed these countries were planning to attack. Russia did not join the League of Nations, which the Soviet newspaper *Izvestia* described as

‘ *. . . a wasps' nest of international intrigue where political sharpers* (cheats) *and thieving diplomatists cheat with marked cards, strangle weak nations, and organise war against the USSR.* **’ (E)**

Lenin's view was that:

‘ *The League is a robbers' den to safeguard the unjust spoils of Versailles.* **’ (F)**

Lenin died in 1924. There was a long struggle for power, but eventually, in 1928, Stalin became ruler of Russia. Stalin continued to improve relations with other countries, signing the Kellogg-Briand Pact in 1928 (see page 17). He believed Russia should concentrate on building up its strength at home; it was not ready to lead a world communist revolution. In any case, he believed communist revolutions were unlikely to occur in European countries for some time. He used the Comintern not for stirring up revolution but for spying and spreading propaganda.

Russia was also concerned about its eastern neighbour, China. In the early 1920s China was in chaos, with several groups struggling for power. Russia supported the Chinese Nationalists (Guomindang) who were gradually gaining control over much of the country. Stalin advised the Chinese Communists to work with the Guomindang. This policy ended in 1927 when the Guomindang attacked the Communists. Then, in 1931, Japan invaded Manchuria in north-eastern China. Stalin at once patched up relations with the Guomindang because he hoped they would prevent or delay further Japanese expansion into China, near the Russian border.

In the 1930s the threat to Russia from Japan and from Hitler's Germany increased. Stalin tried to meet the threat by finding new allies, and in 1934 Russia joined the League of Nations. A modern Russian history book explains this change in Soviet foreign policy:

‘ *Naturally, the Soviet Union saw all the League's weaknesses, its hesitation in stopping aggression and protecting the rights of the victims of aggression. Furthermore, it took into account the anti-Soviet trends in the League's past*

1918–22	Civil War. Lenin introduces 'War Communism' – strict control of the economy to provide supplies for the army
1920	Poland claims territory taken by Russia and invades. Treaty of Riga – Russia agrees to surrender the land
1921	Kronstadt Rising. Sailors and workers at Kronstadt naval base rebel against War Communism. Red Army crushes the revolt. War Communism ends. Lenin introduces 'New Economic Policy' which allows some private ownership and trade
1922	Treaty of Rapallo with Germany
1924	Lenin dies
1927–8	Stalin in control of Communist party
1928	First Five Year Plan – massive programme of industrial development to catch up with capitalist countries
1930	Collectivisation of Russian agriculture begins – strict government control
1932	Famine
1933	Second Five Year Plan
1934	USSR joins League of Nations
1935	Purges of Stalin's opponents begin
1938	Third Five Year Plan

H Russia 1918–38

activities. But . . . the League could to some extent slow down the drift towards war, it could be used to expose and wreck the anti-Soviet aggressive plans. **’ (G)**

(History of Soviet Foreign Policy 1917–45 Moscow, 1969)

H shows the main events in Russia 1918–38. World events in the 1930s and the rise of fascism were to draw Russia more and more into European affairs and eventually into the Second World War.

??????????????

1 What captions might: **a** a Russian textbook; **b** an American textbook, give to pictures **B** and **D**? Explain why you think they would differ.

2 a Why do you think Lenin called the League of Nations 'a robbers' den' (**F**)?
b How had the Russian attitude changed by 1934, according to **G**?
c **G** is *secondary* evidence about Russia in 1934, but it is also *primary* evidence about the Russian view in 1969. How useful are such sources to the historian?

3 a Make notes on how Russia's relations with each of the following countries changed, 1919–34: Germany, Japan, France, Poland.
b If you were an adviser to the Russian government in 1934, how would you suggest they deal with Germany; France; Japan?

6 The League of Nations 1

Before 1914 the great powers had been split into two groups, which seemed to 'balance each other out'. Many people believed that this 'balance of power' between the two groups or alliances would preserve peace. In 1919 the balance of power had gone. People wanted to find a safer way of keeping the peace. Many turned to the idea of 'collective security' – all countries would agree to protect each other, and so peace would be safeguarded.

In 1920 the League of Nations was born. Its headquarters were in Geneva, in Switzerland. **A** shows how the League was organised. **B** shows the aims of the League. These aims, rules and procedures were set out in a document called *The Covenant*, a solemn promise signed by all the member nations. The main purpose of the League, to offer collective security to all its members, was set out in Article 10 of the Covenant:

❝ *The members of the League undertake to respect and preserve against external aggression the territory and existing independence of all members of the League. In case of any such aggression or any threat of danger, the Council shall advise upon the means by which this obligation shall be fulfilled.* ❞ (C)

The Covenant set out the action the League should take to deal with an aggressor in three steps: **1** condemn the country and tell it to stop; **2** impose economic sanctions (ie other members would not trade with the country); **3** use military force (all member countries to provide troops).

The League needed the goodwill and help of every country. But it started with a severe handicap. The USA refused to join, and Germany and Russia were not included until later.

B Aims of the League of Nations

1 To keep world peace by dealing with disputes among nations.
2 To safeguard the independence of countries and their frontiers.
3 To encourage nations to reduce their armaments.
4 To improve living and working conditions for all people.

A Organisation of the League of Nations

The Assembly
Every member of the League had one vote. The assembly met once a year to:
- discuss anything raised by a member
- fix the League's budget
- admit new members
- elect non-permanent members of the Council
A unanimous vote was needed for a decision

The Council
Consisted of four permanent members (Britain, France, Italy, Japan) and non-permanent members (at first three, later ten). It met to deal with emergencies. A majority vote was needed

The Secretariat
An international civil service which prepared reports, kept records and translated documents

The Permanent Court of International Justice
Set up in 1921 at The Hague, Holland. 15 judges gave a decision on disputes between countries – but only when the countries requested this

Agencies and Commissions
A wide range of agencies set up to deal with various problems

International Labour Organisation (ILO)
Tried to improve working conditions and wages

Mandates Commission
The colonies of Germany and Turkey were given to 'caretaker' countries. The Commission kept an eye on the management of these colonies

Minorities Commission
Helped protect people of one nationality forced to live under the rule of a different national group

Other Agencies
Dealt with such problems as drug abuse, slavery, refugees . . . worked to improve world health and education

7 The League of Nations 2: the 1920s

A The opera house in Athens was transformed into living quarters for homeless Greek families

You live in a violent century. At a guess, how many people do you think: died in battle? Died of disease? Became prisoners of war? Were made homeless? . . . as a result of the First World War. You will not find accurate figures for any of these. Some countries did not, or could not, count their dead, homeless or prisoners. But we do know that millions died or were taken prisoner and probably millions more were made homeless.

Clearly there was plenty of work for the League of Nations to do in helping clear up the chaos left by the war. With the help of the Norwegian, Fridtjof Nansen, the League helped return 400 000 prisoners of war to their own countries and found homes for countless refugees (**A**). Other problems the League tackled were the growing traffic in dangerous drugs, the illegal sale of weapons, the sale of women and children as slaves, and the spread of disease. The League also helped raise loans to save Austria from bankruptcy.

The main purpose of the League, however, was to keep the peace. In the 1920s the League had both successes and failures (**B**). Sometimes a problem was settled not by the League but by a Conference of Ambassadors from Britain,

France, Italy and Japan. Their job was to ensure that the decisions in the Peace Treaties were carried out. The Conference was not itself part of the League.

The League was usually successful when a dispute occurred between small, weak countries. When a dispute involved a great power, however, the League often favoured the more important country. The Council of the League dealt with emergencies (see **B** on page 14) and the great powers dominated the Council.

Two of the incidents in **B** show how the League failed to treat the great powers and the small countries equally: the Corfu incident in 1923 and the dispute between Greece and Bulgaria in 1925. Both incidents involved Greece, and the pattern of events on each occasion was very similar.

In the Corfu incident Italy pushed the League aside and used force to get compensation from Greece for the murder of Italian soldiers. But when, in the second dispute, Greece tried to use force, it did not receive compensation for the murder of Greek soldiers but instead had to pay for invading Bulgaria. Italy was a great power; the other great powers in the League were anxious

15

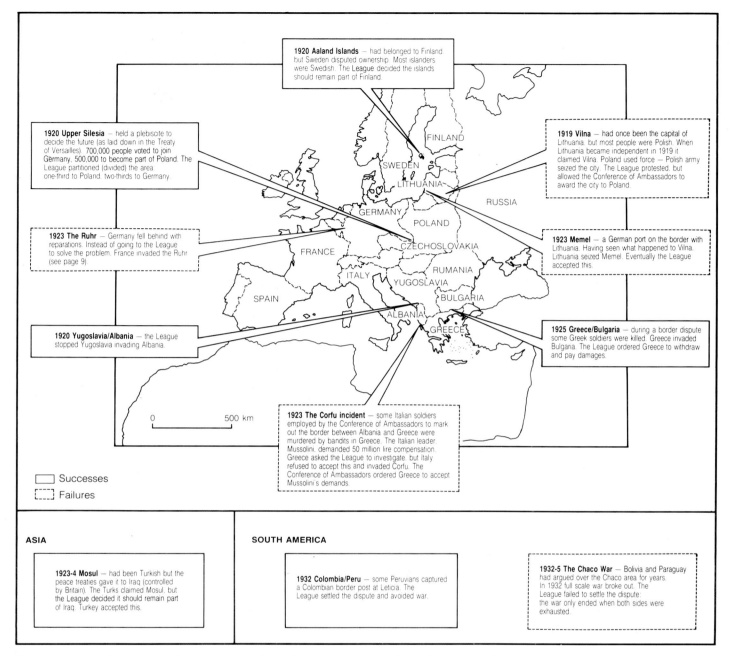

1920 **Aaland Islands** — had belonged to Finland but Sweden disputed ownership. Most islanders were Swedish. The League decided the islands should remain part of Finland.

1920 **Upper Silesia** — held a plebiscite to decide the future (as laid down in the Treaty of Versailles). 700,000 people voted to join Germany, 500,000 to become part of Poland. The League partitioned (divided) the area: one-third to Poland, two-thirds to Germany.

1923 **The Ruhr** — Germany fell behind with reparations. Instead of going to the League to solve the problem, France invaded the Ruhr (see page 9).

1920 **Yugoslavia/Albania** — the League stopped Yugoslavia invading Albania.

1919 **Vilna** — had once been the capital of Lithuania, but most people were Polish. When Lithuania became independent in 1919 it claimed Vilna. Poland used force — Polish army seized the city. The League protested, but allowed the Conference of Ambassadors to award the city to Poland.

1923 **Memel** — a German port on the border with Lithuania. Having seen what happened to Vilna, Lithuania seized Memel. Eventually the League accepted this.

1925 **Greece/Bulgaria** — during a border dispute some Greek soldiers were killed. Greece invaded Bulgaria. The League ordered Greece to withdraw and pay damages.

1923 **The Corfu incident** — some Italian soldiers employed by the Conference of Ambassadors to mark out the border between Albania and Greece were murdered by bandits in Greece. The Italian leader, Mussolini, demanded 50 million lire compensation. Greece asked the League to investigate, but Italy refused to accept this and invaded Corfu. The Conference of Ambassadors ordered Greece to accept Mussolini's demands.

☐ Successes
⌐ ¬ Failures

ASIA

1923-4 **Mosul** — had been Turkish but the peace treaties gave it to Iraq (controlled by Britain). The Turks claimed Mosul, but the League decided it should remain part of Iraq. Turkey accepted this.

SOUTH AMERICA

1932 **Colombia/Peru** — some Peruvians captured a Colombian border post at Leticia. The League settled the dispute and avoided war.

1932-5 **The Chaco War** — Bolivia and Paraguay had argued over the Chaco area for years. In 1932 full scale war broke out. The League failed to settle the dispute; the war only ended when both sides were exhausted.

B Successes and failures of the League of Nations Between 1920 and 1932 nearly 50 political disputes were brought before the League for settlement

C A British cartoon comment on Mussolini's use of force in the Corfu Incident

not to upset the Italians (**C**). Greece, however, was a small, weak country with no powerful friends on the Council.

The Corfu incident was seen as a serious failure for the League in the 1920s. It showed that powerful nations could still bully a less powerful neighbour. **D** is how a modern historian, G Scott (writing in 1973) described the way the League handled the incident:

❝*The settlement made a nasty smell. The Greeks were bitter, the Assembly felt it had been betrayed and that the League had been degraded. Mussolini appeared to have*

E The Geneva Protocol

> **1** Disputes between countries must be settled by arbitration – the League would act as an 'umpire' to sort out the quarrel.
> **2** Countries must accept the decision of the Permanent Court of International Justice.
> **3** Countries in dispute must not prepare for war while the arbitrator was trying to solve the dispute.
> **4** The armed forces of member countries could be used on behalf of the League against an aggressor.

triumphed in his assertion that where a nation was powerful enough it was justified in using force to further its interests and the League had no right to interfere. **(D)**

In 1924 the British Prime Minister, Ramsay Macdonald, drafted the Geneva Protocol (**E**) in an attempt to strengthen the Covenant of the League. But Macdonald fell from power later that year and the new Conservative Government, together with many other countries, refused to sign the Protocol. They did not like the idea of being compelled to accept the League's decisions. The Protocol was abandoned.

A more important step towards peace was the signing of the Locarno Treaties in 1925 (see pages 10–11). Germany and France agreed not to go to war and to bring any disputes to the League. The following year Germany joined the League. A new mood of international co-operation spread across Europe. **F** comes from the diary of the British ambassador to Berlin. It shows the optimism many people felt at the time:

> *15 November 1925 It seems to me difficult to exaggerate the importance of the Reparation Settlement in 1924 and the Treaty of Locarno in 1925.*
> *10 January 1926 Another step forward. Germany has decided to send in her application for admission to the League of Nations.*
> *2 October 1926 ... The war spirit has been quelled, and the possibility of an era of peaceful development opens ... the risk of war between France and Germany is vastly diminished.* **(F)**

Another move towards safeguarding peace came in 1928. The foreign ministers of France and the USA, Briand and Kellogg, drew up the Pact of Paris, otherwise known as the Kellogg–Briand Pact. 65 nations signed the Pact. **G** shows two of the main articles in the Pact.

> *Article 1: The High Contracting Parties declare ... that they condemn recourse (resorting) to war for the solution of international controversies (disputes) and renounce it (give it up) as an instrument of national policy in their relations with one another.*

> *Article 2: The Parties agree that the settlement or solution of all disputes or conflicts of whatever nature which arise among them, shall never be sought except by pacific (peaceful) means.* **(G)**

The problem with the Kellogg–Briand Pact was that it did not provide any way to enforce its terms. This meant it could only work if countries kept their word. In 1931 Japan ignored the agreement (see pages 34–35). The Pact also showed that world leaders still preferred to sign treaties and pacts rather than rely upon the League and the idea of collective security. However, the Pact did help to involve the USA again in international affairs.

As well as safeguarding the peace the other main aim of the League was to encourage countries to disarm. At the Washington Naval Conference in 1922 the USA, Britain and Japan agreed not to build any new battleships and cruisers for ten years, and to keep a ratio of 5:5:3 between their fleets. Apart from this, little real progress was made. The League tried to persuade countries to disarm, but the attempts failed.

??????????????

1 Study **C**
a How are most of the League members reacting to the use of force?
b What has happened to the League's peace plans?
c Which League member is smiling? What reason would that country have for being pleased?

2 What does G Scott mean by 'the settlement made a nasty smell' (**D**)?

3 If **A** and **C** were your only evidence about the League of Nations, what would you say about its work? How would you use the pictures in your account?

4 Copy the chart below and fill it in. For each piece of evidence **A–G**, think: **a** Is the writer/photographer/cartoonist trying to mislead? **b** Are they in a position to know the truth?

Source	Type of evidence	Primary or secondary	Reasons for trusting/not trusting	Any other evidence to support it
A	photo-graph	primary	photographer had no reason to mislead – just showing refugees' conditions	no
C				
...				

5 Draw up two columns, one headed *Successes* and the other *Failures*. Write down in date order what you think were the successes and failures of the League of Nations.

8 The Great Depression

It is almost certain that since you woke up this morning you have made use of something made in another country – perhaps a radio, a car, pens, books, clothes or food. Try to work out how many foreign-made goods you would expect to use in one day. International trade is vital for every country. If that trade collapses, unemployment will rise rapidly. That is what happened in the early 1930s, in the Great Depression or World Slump. The Depression affected millions of people (**A**).

The origins of the Depression lay in the chaos caused by the First World War. The economist J M Keynes criticised the peace-makers at Versailles for failing to understand:

... that the most serious of the problems which claimed their attention were not political or territorial, but financial and economic, and that the perils of the future lay not in frontiers or self-government, but in food, coal and transport. (**B**)

In the 1920s America lent large amounts of money to other countries, especially in Europe. The loans helped these countries to buy and sell goods and thus recover from the war. Many countries, however, while keen to sell goods abroad, at the same time tried to protect their own industries from cheap imported goods by putting up *tariff barriers* (taxes or duties on imports). This is called *protectionism*.

The first countries to protect their industries in this way were the new countries of eastern Europe, such as Hungary and Czechoslovakia. They wanted to achieve *autarky* or self-sufficiency, that is, to make all their own manufactured goods and grow their own food. They believed that this was vital in case war broke out. Can you think why?

A Desperate men and women scavenging for scraps in a Paris marketplace

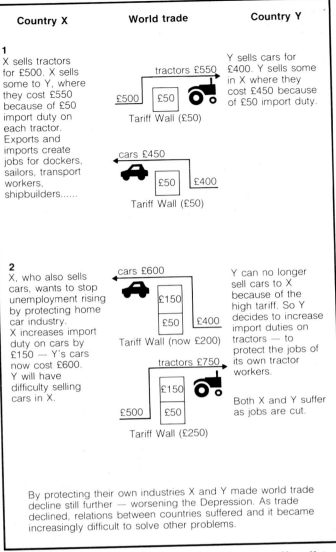

Country X	World trade	Country Y

1
X sells tractors for £500. X sells some to Y, where they cost £550 because of £50 import duty on each tractor. Exports and imports create jobs for dockers, sailors, transport workers, shipbuilders......

tractors £550
£500 | £50
Tariff Wall (£50)

Y sells cars for £400. Y sells some in X where they cost £450 because of £50 import duty.

cars £450
£50 | £400
Tariff Wall (£50)

2
X, who also sells cars, wants to stop unemployment rising by protecting home car industry. X increases import duty on cars by £150 — Y's cars now cost £600. Y will have difficulty selling cars in X.

cars £600
£150
£50 | £400
Tariff Wall (now £200)

Y can no longer sell cars to X because of the high tariff. So Y decides to increase import duties on tractors — to protect the jobs of its own tractor workers.

tractors £750
£150
£500 | £50
Tariff Wall (£250)

Both X and Y suffer as jobs are cut.

By protecting their own industries X and Y made world trade decline still further — worsening the Depression. As trade declined, relations between countries suffered and it became increasingly difficult to solve other problems.

D Protectionism led nations to build up 'tariff walls', and this in turn caused more trade restrictions between nations

Then, in 1922, the US Congress passed the Fordney McCumber Act. This raised taxes on imports, so that foreign goods coming into America were more expensive than American goods. The USA was the greatest trading nation in the world. When the new taxes made it difficult for countries to sell goods to America, world trade suffered. In 1930 America raised import duties still further with the Smoot Hawley Tariff Bill. Other countries replied by raising their tariffs against America. The Argentinian ambassador to the USA explained:

It is perfectly logical that in my country they are thinking of following the example set by countries as advanced as yours and that voices should be heard supporting the adoption of a frankly protective tariff, so that we can make more of the articles which are today imported and so reduce our imports. **(C)**

F Percentage decline in the value of imports and exports, 1929–31

	Imports
USA, Germany	over 50%
Italy, Austria	over 40%
Great Britain, France	over 25%
	Exports
Cuba	over 70%
Brazil	over 60%
Argentina	over 65%
USA	over 50%
Great Britain, Austria	over 40%
France, Italy	over 30%
Germany	over 25%
Russia	under 15%

G Unemployment in millions

	USA	Germany	Britain
1929	1.55	2.48	1.20
1932	12.06	6.12	2.80

D shows the effects of building such a 'Tariff Wall' between nations.

World prices for agricultural goods such as coffee, wheat and sugar fell steadily during the 1920s. Whatever farmers produced, they all faced the same problem:

One American farmer told me he had killed 3000 sheep this fall (Autumn) and thrown them down the canyon, because it cost $1.10 to ship a sheep (to market) and then he would get less than a dollar for it. He said he could not afford to feed the sheep ... so he just cut their throats.
(E)
(Hearings on unemployment: committee of the House of Representatives, 1932)

Low prices meant that countries such as Brazil and Argentina, which depended on selling agricultural goods, could buy little from industrialised countries such as the USA and Britain.

By the late 1920s world trade was in difficulties. Then, in 1929, the American stock market (centred on Wall Street, in New York) crashed (see *Modern America* in this series). American banks could no longer afford to lend any money to Europe. In fact, they wanted countries to repay the money they had lent out. This hit Europe badly. Banks and factories closed. Soon there was a world-wide economic slump (**F**). Millions lost their jobs as industries were ruined (**G**). In many countries the unemployed received little or no help from the government. Many people went hungry. One French woman remembers:

I spent the winter of 1932–33 on the streets, it snowed

Causes	Consequences
1 Tariffs harmed world trade ⟶	increased unemployment and cut investment in industry
2 Low prices for raw materials and agricultural products ⟶	meant farmers and agricultural countries could not afford to buy goods from the industrial countries
3 American loans to Europe were recalled ⟶	increased unemployment in Europe; meant Europe could not afford to buy American goods
4 Large numbers of poor people in all countries, eg Blacks and farmers in America ⟶	many people could not afford to buy the products of the new industries, eg electrical goods, so companies' profits dropped
5 Profits fell ⟶	share prices fell and Wall Street crashed
6 Low prices and low profits ⟶	many farmers and business people were unable to repay bank loans; banks began to go bust and people rushed to take their money out
7 Banks went bust (the first was the Credit-Anstalt in Austria in May 1931) ⟶	industry was unable to borrow money and unemployment increased

J Causes of the Great Depression

and froze, thousands of young men, forced out of their jobs by the crisis, struggled on to their last penny, to the end of their tether then, in despair, abandoned the fight. On the street benches and at tube stations groups of exhausted and starving young men would be trying not to die . . . I saw a child drop a sweet which someone trod on, then the man behind bent down and picked it up, wiped it and ate it.
(**H**)   (Morvan Lebesque, *Chroniques du Canard*, 1960)

K International effects of the Depression

The decline in world trade damaged relations between countries; threats to peace increased and finally resulted in world war. The main effects of the Depression were:

Germany – it led to mass unemployment, disillusionment with the Weimar Republic and the rise of the Nazis, who began to rearm and prepare to expand Germany

Japan – tried to solve its economic problems by invading Manchuria in order to find new markets and raw materials

Italy – Mussolini, the Italian leader, wanted to distract attention from economic problems at home; this encouraged him to invade Abyssinia

USA – was pushed further into isolationism (staying out of problems in Europe). President Roosevelt came to power in 1933 and introduced a 'New Deal', in which he invested government money in large-scale public works such as the huge Tennessee Valley Dam scheme, in order to create more jobs

Britain – feared rearmament and war would further harm its economy, so did not rearm until late 1930s; tried hard to avoid war with Germany

France – felt the effects of the Depression in the mid-1930s; it caused internal political problems and made France delay rearmament

USSR – it had little effect in Russia which had few trade links with the rest of the world

International attempts to end the Depression failed. A World Economic Conference, set up to try and find a solution, collapsed in 1933. **J** shows the main causes of the Depression. **K** shows its world-wide effects.

?????????????????

1 a Explain the following terms: tariff barrier; protectionism; autarky; Fordney McCumber Act.
b How did protectionism affect world trade? How did this contribute to the Depression?

2 According to the Argentinian ambassador (**C**) what was the aim of introducing tariffs?

3 Study **F** and **G**
a Which country suffered the largest rise in unemployment?
b Which three exporting countries do you think exported mainly agricultural products?
c Can you suggest why Russian exports were least affected?
d Which countries suffered a greater decline in imports than in exports?

4 a Which of the points listed in **J** were *direct* causes of the farmer's problems in **E**? Give reasons for your answer.
b Who do you think the writer of **H** would blame for the Depression. Why?

5 In pairs, imagine you are reporters investigating the scene shown in **A**. Produce a report on the plight of the people in the picture, based on the evidence in this section and any other information you can find. What questions would you ask them? What sort of answers might they give? Discuss your reports with another pair.

9 What is fascism?

If you read a newspaper or watch the news on television you will come across many labels used to describe people's political beliefs – labels such as Fascism, Conservatism, Communism, Socialism, left-wing and right-wing. **A** outlines the political 'spectrum'.

This section looks at one of these beliefs – Fascism – as it developed in the Mediterranean countries of Italy, Spain and Portugal in the period between the wars (see map **B**). Originally Fascism was the name given to Mussolini's system of government in Italy between 1922 and 1943. In Germany, the extreme right-wing movement between the wars was the National Socialist, or Nazi, Party. The aggression of these two leading Fascist nations pushed

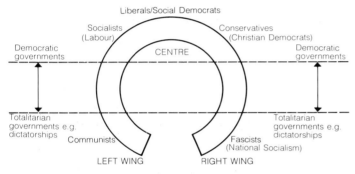

A The 'political spectrum'

The diagram shows that in some ways Fascism (on the extreme right) and Communism (on the extreme left) are similar but in other ways they are very different. Fascism and Communism are both *totalitarian*. The main difference is that Fascism glorifies the nation-state whereas Communism is international and wishes to see the downfall of nation-states.

B Governments in Europe in 1936

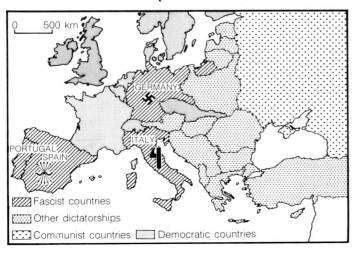

Europe towards the Second World War and revealed the weakness of the League of Nations.

Fascism is not only a party, it is a regime; it is not only a regime but a faith; it is not only a faith but a religion.
(C)   Mussolini

What did Mussolini mean by **C**? It is not easy to explain Fascist ideas and much of what Mussolini wrote and said about his beliefs was confused (see pages 25–29). But it is possible to identify some features common to most Fascist governments (**D**).

Fascism pushed the ideas of nationalism and racialism further than other political movements – as expressed in the popular Fascist slogan 'One State, One Leader, One People'. The features in **D** were given different emphasis and importance in the Fascism of Italy, Spain and Portugal, and the Fascists came to power in different ways in these three countries. In Italy the Fascists seized power quickly. In Spain a long civil war was fought. In Portugal, a university professor was invited to take power, and then adopted Fascist ideas. There were other differences too. By 1939 Mussolini was forming alliances with Hitler, but Spain and Portugal did not follow.

Mediterranean Fascism differed from the Fascism of Hitler's Germany (see pages 40–45). Hitler's beliefs were more brutal and racist. The Nazis believed that their race was superior to any other. In Germany, too, the state had more control over all aspects of life, such as the Church.

D Fascism

1 Obedience to a strong leader

2 No opposition parties allowed

3 Nationalism (a strong feeling for one's country and a wish to make it more powerful)

4 A belief that one's nation deserves to be dominant and that one's race is superior to others

5 Many personal freedoms not allowed – eg the right to say what one believes. Control of the press, broadcasting, education, youth movements, religion, entertainment, the economy and even the family. In a totalitarian state the state has complete (total) power over every aspect of the lives of its members.

6 A large army

7 Hatred of Communism

8 The state, on behalf of the people, controls the means of production (industry and agriculture), distribution (transport), and the banks – so that the nation may become strong

9 A belief that violence should be used, if necessary, to achieve Fascist aims

10 Salazar and Portugal

A

In August 1968 the leader of Portugal, Dr Antonio de Oliveira Salazar (**A**), was sitting in a deckchair, having his hair cut. The deckchair collapsed, and Salazar injured his head. Two months later he collapsed. Doctors diagnosed a blood clot on the brain, and Salazar did not recover. Eventually he died, on 27 July 1970.

Salazar had been leader of Portugal since 1932. He was one of the most unusual leaders in Europe. In 1926 the Portuguese army overthrew the government. In March 1928 the army leader, General Carmona, was elected President. The Portuguese economy was in a mess, and Carmona looked around for a financial expert to sort it out. He chose a university professor, Antonio de Oliveira Salazar, to be his Minister of Finance. Salazar was soon the most important person in Portugal and in 1932 he became Prime Minister. For the next 36 years he ran Portugal as a Fascist dictatorship.

Salazar was rather different from other Fascist leaders. He never wore a military uniform and was by nature a quiet man, who did not favour rousing speeches, parades or displays. Instead, he set out his ideas quietly, in radio broadcasts and in the newspapers. This does not mean that his control was weaker than that of other dictators. As early as 1928 he explained:

❛*I know quite well what I want and where I am going, but let it not be insisted that I shall reach the goal in a few months ... let the country suggest, let it object, and let it discuss but when the time comes for me to give orders I shall expect it to obey.*❜ (**B**)

In July 1930 Salazar formed the National Union, the only political party allowed in Portugal. In 1933 he introduced a new constitution (rules by which a country is governed) called the *Estada Novo* (New State). Under the constitution, free trade unions, strikes and lock-outs were prohibited. The workers were kept under strict control.

Young people had to join the fascist youth movement and wear its 'uniform' of green shirts. Opposition to Salazar was dealt with harshly. The secret police – the PVDE – murdered several hundred of his opponents, and regularly tortured suspects. Salazar even brought in instructors from Nazi Germany and Fascist Italy to teach the PVDE new skills. When one opponent complained as he was being arrested, the head of the PVDE told him:

❛*Your rights. What rubbish. Here I arrest whoever I like and can keep him in prison for as long as I want to. There are only two people I cannot touch, the president and the prime minister.*❜ (**C**)

Salazar was a religious man. His government worked closely with the Catholic Church and gave it an important role in Portuguese life.

The Portuguese economy improved under Salazar's guidance, but some historians argue that he actually held Portugal back. It remained a poor country; most of the population made a living from fishing, making wine, or producing olive oil or cork. Industry was organised in corporations, as in Italy (see pages 24–25).

In his foreign policy, Salazar did not seek close relations with other countries. He was more concerned with Portugal's colonies, which he believed were vital to the country's success. He was determined to keep the colonies, at all costs. When the colony of Goa, in India, was about to be invaded by a much stronger Indian army, Salazar told the Portuguese commander:

❛*I wish no truce and I wish no Portuguese to be taken prisoner. No ship is to surrender. Our soldiers and sailors must conquer or die.*❜ (**D**)

Most of Portugal's colonies were in Africa. Salazar regarded the Africans as racially inferior, and the Portuguese ruled them harshly and often cruelly.

Was Salazar truly Fascist? The extracts in **E** come from some of Salazar's speeches and laws made between 1930 and 1940.

❛*Newspapers ... must be controlled. Communism is the great evil of the age. Like a great family the nation ... requires a head to control it. We make Portuguese nationalism the indestructible base of the New State.*❜ (**E**)

Do you think these were the words of a Fascist leader? The following pages may help you decide.

11 Italy: Mussolini's rise to power

Do you think you would make a good leader for your country? Why? What qualities do you think a good leader should have? **A** describes Benito Mussolini. Did he possess any of these qualities? Do you think he would be a good leader?

In 1919 King Victor Emmanuel III of Italy and his government faced major problems. The war had seriously damaged Italy's economy. Many soldiers could not get jobs when they returned from the war. Prices had risen by 500% since 1915, and there were many strikes and riots. The country itself was divided. The north had industry and was much wealthier than the south, where most people scratched a living as peasants. The government was weak. MPs took bribes, and often behaved like unruly schoolchildren, fighting and throwing paper at each other.

Italy had entered the war on the side of the Allies, mainly because it was promised more territory at the end of the war. But in the Peace Treaties these promises were

A Profile of Mussolini

Name Benito Amilcare Andrea Mussolini

Born 29 July 1883

Mother Schoolteacher

Father Blacksmith

School record Expelled from first school for wounding another boy and leading a protest against school food. Suspended from second for absenteeism, bullying and fighting.

Police record Arrested several times for leading demonstrations against government policy and for writing libellous newspaper articles

Career Qualified as teacher and went to Switzerland. Became interested in Communist ideas of Karl Marx. Supported revolutionary movements and was expelled from Switzerland. Brief spell in the army before returning to teaching. In 1911 became editor of *Avanti* !Forward! the Socialist Party newspaper; argued against spending on weapons in favour of more schools, better roads and medicine. At first opposed Italy fighting in the First World War but soon changed his mind. Left the Socialist Party and set up his own newspaper *Il Popolo d'Italia* (The people of Italy). Joined the army and fought bravely in the trenches. Wounded in an accident in 1917 and returned to edit his newspaper.

Character and interests Interested in revolutionary politics, drink and women. Contracted VD. As a teacher admitted he could not keep order – bribed children with sweets to keep them quiet. An adventurer, a man of action – excited by new ideas, but often impatient and short-tempered.

B Italy and the peace treaties

broken. Italy did not receive Dalmatia and Fiume (**B**) as it had expected. Many Italians were shocked and angry with their Government and with the Allies as a result of the settlement.

In September 1919 Gabriele D'Annunzio, a war hero and poet, led a group of ex-soldiers and seized the port of Fiume. The Italian Government was embarrassed by this action, and a year later forced D'Annunzio to leave Fiume. However, many Italians admired D'Annunzio. They had no confidence in their own government which, they felt, had failed to solve Italy's problems.

Law and order began to break down. Such conditions were ripe for the growth of extreme parties. The left-wing Communist party attracted many people in the industrial cities of the north. In opposition to the Communists, Benito Mussolini set up the extreme right-wing Fascist Party. He organised groups of supporters into fighting groups called Fasci di Combattimento, who wore a uniform of black shirts. The party symbol was the *fasces* (see **B** on page 21) which had been the symbol of power in ancient Rome.

In **C** Italo Balbo, a fascist leader, remembers how he and many other Italians felt at the time:

❛ *When I came back from the war I, like so many others, hated politics and politicians, who, it seemed to me, had betrayed the hopes of the fighting men and had inflicted on*

23

Italy a shameful peace ... Many at that time turned towards Communism which offered a ready and more revolutionary programme. It is certain, I believe, that without Mussolini three-quarters of the Italian youth coming home from the trenches would have become Communists. They wanted a revolution at any cost. **(C)**

Mussolini dreamed of making Italy a great power. He believed the Communists and Socialists stood in the way of achieving this. Moreover, he realised that many factory owners, businessmen, landowners and Catholics would support a right-wing party opposed to Communists and Socialists. The Fascists were ready to use violent methods against their opponents. Mussolini's 'blackshirt' fasci groups attacked the meetings and buildings of Communists and Socialists. They forced some opponents to drink castor oil or eat live toads – others were beaten and killed. Between October 1920 and October 1922 the Fascists murdered an estimated 2000 people. Italo Balbo recalls how he organised operations in the Ravenna area:

I told the chief of police that I would burn down and destroy the houses of all socialists in Ravenna, if he did not provide me with transport. I demanded a whole fleet of lorries ... we went through all the towns and destroyed all the Red buildings, the headquarters of the socialist and communist organisations. Our passage was marked by high columns of fire and smoke. **(D)**

The Fascists won 35 seats in the 1921 elections. In 1922 the Socialists organised a general strike in an attempt to stop the Fascists. This was just what Mussolini wanted, because he could appear as the protector of law and order. The Fascists helped bring down the strike. They broke up workers' demonstrations and factory sit-ins, and helped to run buses and trains and deliver mail. Mussolini announced his support for the King and the Pope and organised a march on Rome to overthrow the Government. He warned:

Fascist Italians! The hour of the decisive battle has come. The army of Blackshirts does not march against the police or army but against the class of stupid and weak-minded politicians, who for four years have not known how to give a government to the nation. Fascism wishes to impose discipline only on the nation as a whole and to give aid to all those forces which will encourage the nation's economic growth and well-being. **(E)**

On 28 October 1922 thousands of Fascist supporters moved towards Rome. But it was not the glorious march that Mussolini later claimed. The marchers were drenched with rain and many were short of food. Meanwhile Mussolini went north to Milan, from where he could escape to Switzerland if things went wrong.

F Mussolini addressing a rally. He adopted the name *Il Duce* (Leader)

The army prepared to defend Rome. On 29 October the Prime Minister, Facta, asked the King for permission to order the army to open fire if necessary. The weak-willed King Victor Emmanuel did not know what to do. He did not trust Facta and could not rely on the army to remain loyal. He was afraid of civil war and worried that he might lose his throne. What would you do? Would you support your Prime Minister in stopping the Fascists, or give in to Mussolini and invite him to become the new Prime Minister?

Victor Emmanuel chose Mussolini. By doing so, he made himself a mere figurehead. From this point, the real power lay with Mussolini (**F**).

Mussolini rushed to Rome. On 30 October he became Prime Minister. His Fascist supporters came to Rome by train and held a victory march. Mussolini had got his way through the threat of violence.

??????????????

1 a Which country do you think Dalmatia became part of (**B**)?
b How did Mussolini's political views change between 1914 and 1919 (**A**)?
c What happened in October 1922?
d Whom did the Blackshirts attack?

2 a Why does Balbo call the Versailles settlement 'a shameful peace' (**C**)?
b Who does Mussolini blame in **E** for Italy's problems?
c What impression of Mussolini do you think the photographer of **F** wanted to give?

3 a Discuss, in pairs or groups, the advice you would give the Italian government in 1919 on how to solve the problems it faced.
b As if you were advisers to the Italian government in 1922, draw up a plan of action for how to deal with the crisis which led to Mussolini taking power.

12 Mussolini in power

'He regarded the mass of the people as easy to deceive and dominate, he thought them to be like children, to be helped and corrected and punished. Mussolini said of the masses. "They are stupid, dirty, do not work hard enough and are content with their little picture shows".' **(A)**

(Dennis Mack Smith *Mussolini*)

In 1922 Mussolini had as much power as a British Prime Minister has today. Parliament and regular elections kept him in check. Mussolini formed a government which included a few Fascists, along with many people from other parties. But on 16 November he warned Parliament:

'I am here to defend and develop the revolution of the Blackshirts. I refused to make an outright conquest as I could have done. With my three hundred thousand armed men ... I could have made this bleak hall a place for my soldiers to sleep. I might have closed parliament altogether and created a government of Fascists alone. I could have done that, but such, at least for the present, has not been my wish.' **(B)**

Mussolini set out to increase his power by gaining control of Parliament and the elections. First he persuaded Parliament to give him full power for a year – so that he could make laws without their consent. Then in 1923 he passed the Acerbo Law. This gave the party which won most votes two-thirds of the seats in Parliament. Elections were held in April 1924 and the Fascists made sure they would win most seats – they stole ballot boxes, voted on behalf of dead men and beat up their opponents. When the results were announced, the Fascists had won 374 of the 554 seats.

In Parliament the Socialist Party leader, Giacomo Matteotti, spoke out against the Fascists. Soon afterwards, in June 1924, Fascist thugs murdered Matteotti. It is not certain that Mussolini ordered the killing, but many Italians blamed him for it and turned against him. It looked as if Mussolini was finished. But on 3 January 1925 he warned Parliament:

'Italy wants peace, tranquillity, calm in which to work. We will give her this tranquillity and calm, by means of love if possible, by force if necessary. You can be sure that within the next 48 hours, the entire situation will become clear ... what I am planning to do is not the result of a wish to govern but solely because of a great love for the fatherland.' **(C)**

In the 48 hours that followed police and Fascist squads moved into action to crush any opposition. Opponents

D How Mussolini took control, 1925–27

1925	● News reports had to be approved by Government
	● Anti-Fascist newspapers closed
	● Fascist officials replaced elected mayors
	● Mussolini head of the Government, with power to make laws without consent of Parliament
1926	● All other political parties banned
	● Trade Unions abolished
	● Opponents imprisoned
1927	● Secret Police force – OVRA – formed

E Thousands attended huge Fascist rallies and parades

G Members of a Fascist youth organisation salute Mussolini

were beaten up or arrested. Anti-Fascist newspapers were closed down. The only non-Fascists in the Government resigned. The King was angry, but he refused to dismiss Mussolini. **D** shows how Mussolini established himself as a dictator (a leader with complete power).

Mussolini was careful to present himself as a father figure who knew what was best for Italy. He was a great showman, and stage-managed speeches and rallies brilliantly. Trumpets, floodlights and stirring words roused huge crowds to chant *Duce! Duce! Duce!* (**E**).

Mussolini created a new system of government headed by a Fascist Grand Council. Then he began to prepare for the 1928 Parliamentary election. He changed the voting system so that only men who belonged to Fascist organisations could vote. Even they could only vote 'Yes' or 'No' to a whole list of candidates chosen by the Grand Council, so there was no real choice. The Fascists won easily. Mussolini had Parliament in his pocket and few people dared to oppose him.

Controlling the people

The Fascists set out to control people's minds and behaviour. This started at school – **F** shows how one primary school textbook described the ideal pupil:

❝Teacher: *What is the twenty-eight of October?*
Bruno: *It is the anniversary of the March on Rome. The*

Fascists in their Blackshirts enter Rome and put everything in order. Then the Duce arrives and says, "Go away all nasty Italians who do not know how to do things for the good. Now I will see to putting everything right! Long live Italy!"
Teacher: *Good. All of you know already what Fascism is and what Benito Mussolini has done for Italy. On October 28th 1922, there began his great work of renewal, which is not yet finished, but which has changed the face of Italy.* ❞
(**F**)

Schoolchildren began the day by repeating the Fascist Creed which began '*I believe in the genius of Mussolini . . .*' On every classroom wall hung two pictures, one of Jesus Christ and one of Mussolini. Every pupil had to read the *Libro Unico* (single book) which was full of stories about the glories of Fascism and the god-like qualities of Il Duce.

Children were expected to join youth movements. At the age of four, boys could join the *Sons of the She Wolf* and at eight the *Balilla,* in which they did military training. For girls there was the *Little Italian Girls* which trained them for motherhood. At 14, both boys and girls could join the *Avanguardisti* and then go on to the *Young Fascists* (**G**).

Everyone was bombarded with propaganda. The Minculpop (Ministry of Popular Culture) made sure that newspapers, cinemas, theatres, books and radio all put forward Mussolini's message. Even leisure time was controlled by the Dopolavoro, which organised sports, entertainment and holidays for workers.

The Church

One challenge to Mussolini's control over Italians was the Roman Catholic Church. The Church had been on bad terms with the Italian state ever since 1860, when Church lands were taken over. Many Italians were good Catholics; Mussolini realised that the support of the Pope would increase his control. Although Mussolini did not believe in Christianity he tried to appear to be a good Catholic. In 1929 he signed the Lateran Treaties and Concordat with the Catholic Church (**H**).

H Terms of the Lateran Treaty

> **1** The Vatican City to be an independent state, with its own army, police and post office.
> **2** 1 750 000 million lire to be paid to the Church as compensation for the land lost in 1861.
> **3** Roman Catholicism to be the only state religion; religious education to be compulsory at school.
> **4** The Pope would accept the King and Mussolini as rulers of Italy.

This alliance made Mussolini more respectable. Many Italian Catholics now felt they could also be loyal Fascists. Mussolini's view was:

❮*The Pope? He is one of my helpers. He looks after the dead. I look after the living. To him the kingdom of souls. To me the kingdom of the living.* ❯ (**J**)

The economy

Italy needed to be wealthy if it was to become a leading world power. Mussolini needed to control the economy and solve many economic problems. He began by making Italy a 'Corporate state'. In 1925 trade unions were abolished and strikes outlawed. Workers and bosses were brought together in Corporations. By 1936 there were 22 Corporations, each dealing with a main occupation. The Mining Corporation, for example, included everyone involved in the mining industry. With the help of a Fascist chairman, the workers and bosses in the Corporation would meet to agree on wages, working conditions and prices.

Each Corporation sent delegates to the National Council of Corporations. This was meant to help Mussolini run the economy, but he usually ignored its advice. The idea of the 'Corporate state' was a sham. In fact the bosses always had more power in the Corporations than the workers, and large companies like Fiat did much as they liked. Also, many of the Corporations were corrupt.

K shows the main 'battles' in Mussolini's campaign to solve Italy's economic problems. In 1927 a huge programme of public works began. Hospitals, schools, sports stadia and *autostrada* (motorways) were built and the main railway lines were electrified. But Mussolini never solved the real economic problems in Italy – he was like a doctor trying to treat deep wounds by sticking plasters over them! Mussolini's foreign adventures in Abyssinia and Spain (see pages 28–29) put a further strain on the economy. The true weakness of Fascist Italy was shown in the Second World War, when the Italian war machine quickly ground to a halt and had to be rescued by the German army.

K Mussolini's economic policy 1925–39

> *The battle for grain* – aim to raise wheat production so that Italy would not have to import wheat. Farmers were encouraged to switch from other crops, but often they grew wheat on soils more suited to other kinds of produce. More wheat grown, but production of fruit and dairy products declined and valuable exports lost.
>
> *The battle for land* – marshes and swamps to be drained. Most famous was the Pontine Marshes near Rome. Many schemes begun but few finished.
>
> *The battle for the lira* – aim to restore the value of Italian currency (the lira). Made Italian goods expensive for foreign countries to buy, so trade declined. Caused some unemployment.
>
> *The battle for births* – Mussolini believed that the more Italians there were the more powerful Italy would be. Rewarded couples with many children and heavily taxed bachelors. On Christmas Day 1933 mothers with 14 or more children had the honour of meeting Mussolini.

?????????????????

1 Make notes on the meaning of: Acerbo Law; Balilla; Dopolavoro; Il Duce; Minculpop.

2 a Which sentences in Mussolini's speech (**C**) would a Socialist opponent *least* believe, and why?
b Mussolini liked to be thought of as the ideal leader. What qualities do you think he wanted to show in each of **B**, **C**, and **J**?

3 In pairs, write captions for photographs **E** and **G** as if you were *either* a supporter *or* an enemy of Mussolini in 1938. Discuss your captions with your partner.

4 Divide your page in half. On one side, make out a diary for a day in your school life. On the other side, put down what you think you would have been doing at the same times if you had been an Italian school pupil in 1938.

5 Write *either* a page for an Italian school textbook in 1938 explaining Italy's economic success *or* a report for an Italian newspaper (dated 1938) on Mussolini's achievements at home since he came to power.

13 Mussolini's foreign policy

Learn and then shout these slogans:

'It is a crime not to be strong!
War is to men what childbearing is to women!
Nothing has ever been won in history without bloodshed!' (**A**)

Do you think these are the words of a man of peace or an aggressive dictator? What do they suggest about this man's attitude towards other countries? Mussolini was very good at thinking of such slogans. He hoped they would stir up a desire for war in the Italian people. Mussolini dreamed of building a new Roman Empire. **B** shows his attempts to spread Italian influence in the Mediterranean. In 1925 Mussolini signed the Locarno Treaties and in 1928 the Kellogg–Briand Pact. In both, the signing countries promised not to use force to solve international disputes. Mussolini signed not because he believed in the treaties but because he thought it would show that Italy was playing a vital role in world affairs.

In the early 1930s Mussolini appeared to be a vital ally for Britain and France against the growing power of Nazi Germany. He feared a German takeover of Austria, Italy's northern neighbour. In 1934 Mussolini warned Hitler that he would fight to protect Austria, and moved Italian troops up to the border. Hitler backed down. Leaders from Britain and France met Mussolini at Stresa, in Italy, and the three nations formed the 'Stresa Front' against the growing threat from Germany.

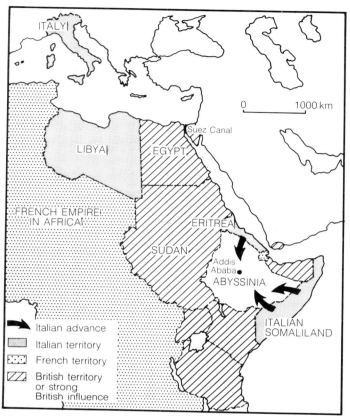

C Italy and Abyssinia 1934–36

Legend:
- Italian advance
- Italian territory
- French territory
- British territory or strong British influence

B Mussolini's foreign policy

1922	Mussolini lends money to Albania; tries to control its economy
1923	Corfu Incident – Mussolini gets his own way against Greece and League of Nations (see p 15)
1925	Mussolini attends Locarno Conference
1928	Italy signs Kellogg–Briand Pact
1934	Italy defends Austria against threat from Germany
1935	*April* Stresa Conference
	Oct Italy invades Abyssinia
	Dec Hoare–Laval Pact fails
1936	Mussolini declares war against Abyssinia won
1939–9	Italian 'volunteers' sent to help Franco in Spanish Civil War
1937	Rome–Berlin Axis – Italy joins Anti-Comintern Pact and leaves League of Nations
1938	Mussolini agrees to Germany taking control of Austria. Munich Conference
1939	*April* Italy occupies Albania
	May Pact of Steel with Germany

Soon, however, everything changed. Mussolini increasingly wanted to fight a war. He believed this would help Italians forget their problems at home. It would also win the coal, iron and oil Italy lacked. Mussolini wanted to add Abyssinia (now called Ethiopia) to the Italian Empire. Abyssinia was sandwiched between the Italian colonies of Eritrea and Somaliland (**C**). It was an independent country, ruled by the Emperor Haile Selassie. It was also a member of the League of Nations, and therefore one of the small countries which the collective security of the League was meant to protect.

For Mussolini, gaining Abyssinia would be a chance to win the glory he so desperately wanted. In 1896 the Abyssinians had defeated the Italian army at the Battle of Adowa. Mussolini wanted revenge for this humiliation. In 1934 Italian troops stationed in Somaliland argued with Abyssinian troops, and finally fought them at Wal Wal in Abyssinia. Then in 1935 the Italians invaded. The Italian soldiers used tanks, poison gas, bombs and flame-throwers against Abyssinian troops armed with spears and outdated rifles.

D 'The awful warning'
France and England (together): *We don't want you to fight*
But, by jingo, if you do
We shall probably issue a joint
memorandum
Suggesting a mild disapproval of
you.

At first the Abyssinians managed to hold the Italian attack. But eventually the Italians pushed forward. Haile Selassie appealed to the League of Nations for help. Britain and France, two leading members of the League, could have stopped Italy by closing the Suez Canal to Italian ships – cutting the Italian supply route to Abyssinia (see **C**). Instead they agreed with the rest of the League to impose certain economic sanctions on Italy. (**D**). These measures had little effect, because they did not include steel, oil and coal, which were vital to the Italian war effort.

Not all Italians had been in favour of the expensive, far-off war. But the sanctions caused Italians to rally in support of Mussolini. **E** is a school dictation exercise from the time. It shows how Fascist propaganda about the war was used to influence the young.

❛*We have shown the world that we are the strong ones, the just ones, the best ones. The fifty-two sanctionist nations refused us bread, iron, gold, coal and cloth; we found it all anyway: bread from the fields of Italy. Iron from the houses of Italy. Black coal from the mines and forests of Italy. They wanted to humiliate us, but our victory and sacrifice has raised us above them.* ❜ (**E**)

In December 1935 Britain and France tried to stop the war in Abyssinia. The British Foreign Secretary, Sir Samuel Hoare, and the French Prime Minister, Pierre Laval, put forward a secret plan. In this they agreed that Italy would keep two-thirds of Abyssinia. But when news of the agreement got out it was so unpopular with the people of Britain and France that both Hoare and Laval had to resign. The plan was dropped.

In 1936 Haile Selassie again asked the League for help:

❛*I claim that justice which is due to my people and the assistance promised it eight months ago. That assistance has been constantly refused me. I assert that the problem submitted to the Assembly today is a much wider one than that of the situation created by Italy's aggression ... It is the very existence of the League of Nations that is at stake.* ❜ (**F**)

In May 1936 the Italians captured the capital of Abyssinia, Addis Ababa. After that the war was soon over. Mussolini claimed a great victory:

❛*Italy has her Empire – a Fascist Empire. An Empire of peace, because Italy desires peace, for herself and for all men, and she decides upon war only when it is forced upon her.* ❜ (**G**)

The Abyssinian crisis dealt a death blow to the League of Nations which was now ignored as a peace-keeping body. Italy's friendship with Britain and France also suffered. The Stresa Front fell apart, and Mussolini moved towards closer links with Germany.

Mussolini was confident that more victories would follow. He looked around the Mediterranean for a further chance to extend Italian territory and influence. The civil war in Spain offered him that chance.

??????????????

1 Study map **C**
a Which Italian colonies are shown?
b Which European power dominated this part of East Africa?
c If the Suez Canal had been closed, was there any other route by which Italy could send supplies to Abyssinia? If so, how?

2 a How does the cartoonist of **D** portray Britain and France?
b What is his view of their policy over Abyssinia? Give reasons for your answer.

3 Why did Haile Selassie say 'the very existence of the League is at stake?' (**F**)?

4 Imagine you are an adviser to Mussolini in 1936. Draft a speech for him to give to his troops before the invasion. Mention: Fascism; glory; empire; Britain; modern weapons; Haile Selassie; Battle of Adowa.

14 The Spanish Civil War 1: Causes

In 1934 Louis Fischer, a journalist, described a recent visit to Spain.

A peasant told me: "I am not hungry today, I ate my cat." I thought he was joking. But the villagers nodded in agreement. A woman of 27, who had five living children and looked 55, said: "Recently a horse fell dead on the road and we ran out and cut strips of meat from it."

I went into a least a dozen huts and looked for food supplies. No family had sugar. In one earthen house I found two small bunches of onions, four potatoes, a small, half-filled bottle of vegetable oil, and nothing else: no bread. (A)

Spain was a very backward country. Most people were very poor. There were, however, a few extremely rich people. In 1936 a civil war broke out in Spain. It ended in victory for a government with beliefs similar to those of the Fascists in Italy. In many ways, this war was a fight between those who had little and those who had much. **B** shows the groups of people involved.

Which groups of people in **B** would want to change the way the country was run? Which groups would want to keep things unchanged? This will give you a rough idea of the two sides in the civil war. But of course the division was not so clear-cut. Many Spaniards, both rich and poor, were loyal Catholics. So they supported the Church against those who wanted to change things.

In the 1930s Spain had a wide range of different political groups:

Left-wing groups: communists, socialists and anarchists. These groups wanted to make great changes, in particular

B Groups involved in the Spanish Civil War

1 Very rich owners of enormous ranches or farms, called *latifundia*. 72% of land owned by just 5% of people
2 The Catholic Church – very rich and powerful.
3 The large army – provided careers for the sons of the rich
4 The civil guard (armed police force)
5 Over 2.5 million peasants (*braceros*). Very poor, had no land and were hired by the day to work on latifundia. Sometimes starving; kept under control by army and civil guard.
6 Poorly-treated workers in the few industrial areas, such as Bilbao, Barcelona.
7 Separatists, especially Basques and Catalans, who wanted independence for their areas.

C Spain 1902–36: The steps to civil war

1902	Alfonso XIII becomes King of Spain
1923	Primo de Rivera stages bloodless coup. Rules as dictator but allows Alfonso to remain King. Popular at first, begins to modernise Spain.
1929–30	World slump hits Spain. Unemployment and economic problems. Rivera loses support of army and resigns
1931	*April* Alfonso abdicates. *14 April* Second Republic declared *June* New government elected, led by Manuel Azana. Introduces reforms: Church property confiscated; Church control of schools ended; army reduced; Basques and Catalans promised own governments; plans to split up latifundia and give land to peasants
1933	*Dec* Right-wing government elected, led by Jose Robles. Strikes and riots. Armed clashes with police. Industrial workers in Northern Asturies rebel – brutally put down by army
1936	*Feb* Elections between Popular Front (left-wing – Communists, Socialists, Anarchists, Republicans) and National Front (right-wing Catholics, Monarchists, Landowners Party, Falange/Fascists). Popular Front win 256 seats, National Front 143 *July 17–18* Army rebels and joins with local fascist groups to overthrow government

to take all land from the rich and the Church and share out Spain's wealth more fairly. The Communists believed this would be achieved by violent revolution, as had happened in Russia. The Socialists wanted to bring about changes through Parliament. Anarchists felt it was best done by having no central government at all. All three parties had most support from the peasants and workers.

Right-wing groups: the Church, the army, monarchists (supporters of royalty who wanted the return of the King) and the new Spanish fascist party, the Falange. These groups all wanted to protect their wealth and power (see **B**).

Centre groups: Liberals who wanted to create a modern democracy like that of Britain or France, by gradual change.

C shows the steps which led up to the outbreak of civil war. In 1936 the 'Popular front', made up of left-wing parties, won the election. They planned to bring back the reforms introduced by Azana's government in 1931.

These reforms would break the hold that the army, the Church and landowners had over Spain. Peasants and anarchists had already begun to seize land for themselves. Law and order was breaking down. Faced with this threat, the army decided to take action. Led by General Francisco Franco (**D**) it rebelled against the Government. Franco's army was in Morocco but he brought it to Spain. There he appealed to the Spaniards:

❝*Spaniards! To whoever feels a holy love of Spain, to those in the Army and Navy . . . to those who have sworn to defend Spain from her enemies, the Nation calls you to her defence. Are we to abandon Spain to her enemies? . . . No!*❞ (**E**)   (Speech on 19 July 1936)

Franco was supported by the Church, the rich land-owners and the Falange. He adopted the Falange's ideas and soon took it over. Together the rebels were known as the Nationalists.

The Government armed many ordinary Spaniards – including liberals, socialists, communists and anarchists – who wanted to stop the army takeover. Militia groups were quickly formed (**F**). A reporter later remembered:

❝*Thousands of trade unionists employed and unemployed, dock workers, labourers, shop assistants, office workers were flocking to the recruiting depots for the militia. Girls were as welcome as boys. They were being packed into trucks and wagons and rushed off to the fronts.*❞ (**G**)
(Robert Kisch *They Shall Not Pass*, 1974)

D General Franco at lunch on the battlefield, January 1939

F Government militiamen in 1936

??????????????

1 A was written by a left-wing journalist. How does this affect its value for the historian? What problems might he/she have in using it as historical evidence?

2 a Who is Franco appealing to in **E**?
b What beliefs or emotions is he using in his appeal?
c How effective do you think this speech would be in winning Franco support?

3 a What sort of people joined the militia groups (**G**)?
b What reasons might they have for supporting the Government (see **B**)?

4 a It is July 1931. You are in a village in the Basque country. The villagers are meeting to discuss the Azana reforms. Split into groups. Each group takes on the role of one of the following: a rich land-owning family; the local Catholic priests; a family of army officers; a policeman; a family of peasants; a poor industrial worker returning from Barcelona; a group of Basque separatists.
b You return to the village five years later. There is a new debate about which side to join in the Civil War. Form the same groups and discuss what each of you will do.

5 Plan and write an essay on the question 'Why did civil war break out in Spain in 1936?' (Mention: rich and poor; different political groups; Azana's reforms in 1931; government of Jose Robles; the 1936 elections; the army and Franco.)

15 The Spanish Civil War 2

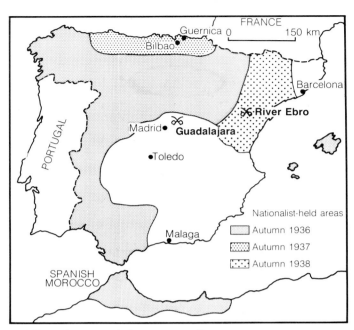

A The advance of the Nationalists

Would you take up a rifle and fight in a civil war for something you believed in? Young people of your age died fighting in the Spanish Civil War. Which side would you have chosen – Nationalist or Republican?

Foreign involvement

By August 1936 Spain was divided (**A**). The Nationalists, led by Franco, appealed to Mussolini and Hitler for help. Mussolini sent 50000 men, together with tanks and aircraft. Hitler sent 16000 men and the Condor Legion of the German Airforce. Mussolini hoped that Franco would prove a useful ally in helping Italy dominate the Mediterranean. Hitler hoped a long war in Spain would distract Mussolini's attention from a German takeover of Austria, and he saw Franco as a valuable ally against France. He also used the Spanish war to test out German weapons, men and tactics.

The Republicans appealed for help to the League of Nations, but the League no longer had the power or the will to do anything. The only aid the Republic received came from Soviet Russia, which sent weapons and advisers. Britain and France did not want to get involved. They set up a Non-Intervention Committee to try and make sure that no foreign aid went to either side. The Committee had little effect, since Germany, Italy and Russia ignored it, although they were members.

Many people in many countries wanted to stop the spread of fascism. Volunteers flocked to join the International Brigade and fight for the Republic. One of them was Jim Lardner, an American. He explained:

❝*I resigned my job and joined the International Brigade. It seems unnecessary to set down my reasons for joining . . . The cause is so plainly a worthy one that young men should ask themselves what reason there is to stay out of the struggle. The situation boils down to this: Fascism must be removed from the world for the good of all; the only way fascism can be removed is to fight it.*❞ (**B**)

(*Volunteer for Liberty*, 1938)

Fewer people volunteered to help Franco. One man who did was Peter Kemp. Much later (1969) he explained why:

❝*It seemed clear to me that the greatest danger to Europe was Communism, and that the Communists were – or soon would be – in control of the Republican government . . . if you hold deep beliefs you must be prepared to defend them, if necessary in battle.*❞ (**C**)

The Spanish Civil War pushed Italy and Germany into a closer friendship and helped make clear the differences between the fascist countries, on one side, and, on the other, communist Russia and democratic countries.

The fighting

In 1936 the Nationalists took control of half of Spain (see **A**). The Republicans held the capital, Madrid, and this soon became the focal point of the war. **D** shows the course of the fighting.

Much of the war was fought in lines of trenches, but there were new dangers, especially for civilians. In 1937 the German Condor Legion bombed and destroyed the town of Guernica. Soon after the attack, an Australian journalist, Noel Monks, arrived in the town:

❝*I was immediately pressed into service by some soldiers collecting charred bodies. Some of the soldiers were sobbing like children. In my message I told the facts about the bombing of Guernica as follows: At 4pm some 40 German and Italian aeroplanes came . . . By 7pm there was no Guernica. About a thousand men, women and children lay in pieces among the market place, in the gutters and under the ruins where their homes had been . . . friends picked up some dud incendiary bombs branded with the German eagle.*❞ (**F**)

It was a bitter war, in which both sides committed atrocities and executed prisoners. A British reporter described the fate of one group of Republicans captured by the Nationalists.

"The Reds" are still being rounded up. They were young, mostly peasants and mechanics. At 4 am they are turned out into the bull ring. There the machine-guns await them. After the first night the blood was supposed to be palm deep. I don't doubt it. Eighteen hundred men – there were women too – were mowed down there in some twelve hours. There is more blood than you would think in 1800 bodies. (**G**)

(*News Chronicle* 3 September 1936)

The Republicans did not treat their prisoners any better. The war left many parts of Spain in ruins, with many people homeless and 600 000 dead (**H**).

H Part of Madrid after heavy German bombing raids

D The Spanish Civil War 1936–39

1936 *17 July* Army in Spanish Morocco rebels against the Republican Government; *18–20 July* Nationalists in Spain rebel; *26 July* German and Italian aircraft arrive in Spanish Morocco
Sept Nationalists capture Toledo
Oct First Russian arms arrive. Franco becomes head of state of Nationalist Spain
Nov International Brigade helps defend Madrid
By the end of 1936 Nationalists control half Spain

1937 *Feb* Malaga falls to Nationalists
Mar Italian troops defeated at Guadalajara
April German Condor Legion bombs Guernica
June Nationalists capture Bilbao
Sept Nyon Conference in Switzerland. Britain and France agree to operate naval patrols in Mediterranean to protect ships from attack by (Italian) submarines
By the end of 1937 Nationalists have captured northern coastal strip (defeating Basques)

1938 *April* Nationalists cut Republican Spain in half
June Republicans launch major attack across Ebro
Nov Nationalists push Republicans back over Ebro

1939 *Jan* Barcelona surrenders to Nationalists
Feb Azana into exile in France. Republican resistance in Catalonia ends
Mar Nationalists enter Madrid. Republicans put up last desperate defence
April Civil War ends in victory for Franco (**E**).

E Why the Nationalists won

1 Most of the army and civil guard joined the Nationalists
2 They received much more foreign help than the Republicans
3 They controlled the richer agricultural areas
4 They had one clear leader, Franco – a good soldier and in full control
5 The Republicans were not united. Different groups (especially the communists and anarchists) argued and sometimes fought each other
6 At first the Republican army mainly consisted of untrained peasants and workers struggling with poor equipment.

?????????????????

1 What were: the Non-Intervention Committee; the Condor Legion; the International Brigade?

2 Read **B** and **C**. What different reasons do the writers give for joining each side? In what ways do these sources contradict each other?

3 a Is **F** primary or secondary evidence of: the attack; the effects of the attack?
b What does the writer of **G** mean by 'the Reds'?

4 Some historians argue that the Condor Legion did not destroy Guernica, but that the Republicans wrecked it for their own reasons. What is there in **F** to contradict this idea? (Remember that the writer did not actually see the attack.)

5 a Place reasons 1–6 in **E** in what you think were their order of importance for Franco's victory. Explain your first and last choice.
b Which of reasons 1–6 had short-term effects on the Republican war effort, and which had long-term effects?

6 'In many ways the Spanish Civil War was an "international war"' Do you agree? Write an essay arguing for or against this view. (Mention: Italy; Germany; Russia; International Brigade; Non-Intervention Committee; Nyon Conference.)

16 Japan and the League of Nations 1930–33

Between 1930 and 1945 millions of Japanese died with a prayer on their lips: '*Banzai*' – meaning 'May the Emperor live 10000 years.' To the Japanese, their Emperor was a god-king. In 1926 Crown Prince Hirohito became Emperor. According to one modern historian, Hirohito was:

> *. . . a formidable war leader: tireless, dedicated, meticulous, clever and patient. He had inherited from his great-grandfather a mission, which was to rid Asia of white men. Since his people were reluctant and backward, he . . . skilfully manipulated them for 20 years in order to prepare them for their task.* (**A**)

(David Bergamini *Japan's Imperial Conspiracy*, 1971)

Not everyone agrees with this view of Hirohito. Some argue that he was a quiet, shy man whose main interest was studying fungi, and who left his generals and admirals to manage the Empire.

In 1931 Japan faced serious problems at home (**B**). The Army leaders and Emperor Hirohito believed that the answer to these problems lay in enlarging the Japanese Empire. They decided to invade Manchuria (see map **C**). Manchuria was part of China, but China at that time was weak and split by civil war. Manchuria could supply Japan with some of the raw materials its industry needed, and it would provide a market for Japanese goods. Japan had controlled Korea and the area of Kwantung, around Port Arthur, since 1905. It also owned the South Manchurian Railway which ran from Korea to Mukden (Shenyang) and had the right to send Japanese troops to guard it.

B Japan's domestic problems

> **1** Industries needed raw materials such as coal, iron, oil, tin and rubber, but Japan was not self-sufficient in these materials.
> **2** Japan's industry was hit hard by the Depression – by 1931 half its factories were idle. The demand for Japan's main export, silk, fell sharply. In 1931 the price paid was only one third of the 1925 price. So Japan had a struggle to buy the goods it needed.
> **3** Many peasants were ruined as the price they got for agricultural produce fell. They moved to the cities in search of work.
> **4** The government had difficulty controlling the power of the army and the *Zaibatsu* (large industrial companies).

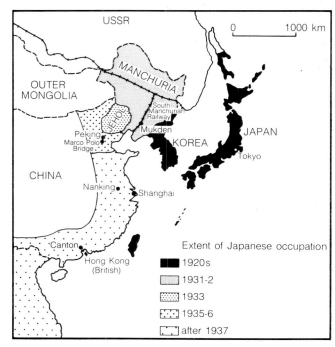

C Japanese expansion in the 1930s

The Japanese army prepared to seize Manchuria. It ignored orders from the Japanese Government to stop. In September 1931 there was an explosion on the South Manchurian Railway. In a statement on 24 September, the Japanese claimed

> *. . . a detachment of Chinese troops destroyed the tracks of the South Manchurian Railway near Mukden, and attacked our railway guards at midnight on 18 September.* (**D**)

The Chinese account said that:

> *At ten o'clock last night, Japanese railway guards picked a quarrel by blowing up a section of the railway near Mukden, and then accused the Chinese military of having done this . . . At 5.30 am large groups of Japanese soldiers began entering the city of Mukden.* (**E**)

(Official Chinese report, 19 September)

Who was telling the truth? **F** is a Japanese photograph said to show the damage to the railway line. Later evidence revealed that the Japanese faked the incident. A Japanese lieutenant

> *(buried) 42 cubes of yellow blasting powder five feet away from the tracks . . . carefully so that they would throw a lot of dirt but would cause no real damage . . . the*

F A Japanese photograph of the damage to the South Manchurian Railway, said to be the work of the Chinese

Japanese claimed that Chinese soldiers had set the blast and destroyed over a yard of track. ❯ (G)

(David Bergamini *Japan's Imperial Conspiracy* 1971)

Nevertheless, the incident gave the Japanese army the excuse it wanted. An official Japanese report explained:

❮ *In order to prevent an imminent disaster, the Japanese army had to act swiftly . . . the Japanese Government has no territorial designs on Manchuria.* ❯ (H)

Within four days the Japanese controlled an area of 200 miles around Mukden. China appealed to the League of Nations. The Chinese leader, Chiang Kaishek, told his people:

❮ *The challenge thrown to us is also a challenge to all nations. The League of Nations was established to prevent war and bring collective action into play to stop aggression. We have immediately . . . asked the League to obtain as a first step the immediate withdrawal of the invaders. The Council of the League is dealing with the matter at Geneva.* ❯ (J)

The Japanese Government told the army to withdraw, but it continued to advance. By December 1931 the Japanese controlled all of Manchuria. The League of Nations sent a Commission to Manchuria to investigate the facts, led by the British Lord Lytton. It was not easy for the Commission to find out the truth. Lord Lytton pointed out that the Japanese police

❮ *kept away witnesses, and many Chinese were frankly afraid of even meeting members of our staff. Interviews were usually arranged in secrecy.* ❯ (K)

In February 1932 Japan announced that Manchuria was an independent state, and renamed it Manchukuo. Pu Yi,

the last Chinese Emperor (who had been overthrown by the Chinese themselves in 1912) was made ruler of the new state. But he was only a figurehead. Manchuria was really run by the Japanese army.

One way in which the Japanese controlled the Chinese, and made them pay for the cost of keeping the army and officials in Manchuria was through the drug trade. Japanese agents sold vast quantities of opium, heroin and cocaine to the Chinese, and made huge profits. It was common for workers to go without food, keeping themselves going by smoking opium until they simply dropped dead.

In November 1932 Lord Lytton made his report to the Council of the League of Nations. In it, he condemned Japan and recommended that the Japanese should be asked to leave Manchuria. The Assembly accepted his report in February 1933, but Japan rejected it and left the League. While the League was voting on Lytton's report, Japanese troops invaded Jehol province (see map C).

The only great powers with any military presence in the Far East were the USA and Britain. The USA was not a member of the League. Britain did not have the power to stop Japan, and in any case the British government did not want to endanger trade with Japan.

This was the first of several aggressive acts by different countries during the 1930s which the League failed to deal with effectively. It soon became clear that when faced with a great power determined to get its own way, the League was virtually powerless.

??????????????

1 a Does the evidence in this chapter support or disagree with the view of Hirohito in **A**?
b How was the Japanese claim about their plans for Manchuria (**H**) later shown to be untrue?

2 Study **F**
a Do any of the rails or sleepers appear to be damaged?
b Would the track be easy or difficult to repair?
c What evidence might you expect to find if a railway line was blown up?
d Who do you think took the photograph, and why?
e What are the advantages and disadvantages of using photographs as historical evidence?

3 a Is **G** primary or secondary evidence?
b What did Chiang Kaishek mean in the first sentence of **J**?
c What reasons might: the Japanese; Lord Lytton; give for the behaviour of the Japanese police (**K**)?

4 As if you were a backer of the Japanese government, produce an argument supporting the Japanese behaviour towards China and the League of Nations, 1931–34.

17 Japanese aggression 1933–41

A Ruins in Shanghai after the Japanese attack, February 1938

Today the Japanese call the years 1931–41 the *Kurai tanima* (dark valley). It was a time when the army had too much power. Japan's success in Manchuria in 1931 strengthened the power of the army, and of those politicians who wanted to expand the Japanese Empire.

Within the army there were two opposing groups. One group, supported by the Emperor Hirohito, wanted to strike south and invade the rest of China. The other group wanted to strike north and attack Russia. Those in favour of moving southwards won. In July 1937 Japanese troops clashed with Chinese troops at Marco Polo Bridge, south of Beijing (Peking).

The Japanese said the war began accidentally – because the Japanese commander thought one of his men had been captured by the Chinese (in fact the soldier was relieving himself in nearby bushes). This incident sparked off a Japanese attack, and this soon developed into a full-scale war (**A**). Was it really an accident? Evidence suggests that the Japanese had carefully planned the incident to give them an excuse to invade the rest of China.

Japanese troops soon captured most of north-east China and then went on to take Shanghai (see map on page 34). A British journalist visited part of Shanghai after the attack:

> *There is hardly a building standing which has not been gutted by fire. Smouldering ruins and deserted streets . . . the only living creatures being dogs unnaturally fattened by feasting on corpses. Of a population of about 100000, I saw only five Chinese.* (**B**)

The Japanese soldiers took a delight in killing. They even made it a competition. A Japanese newspaper reported:

> SUB-LIEUTENANTS IN RACE TO FELL 100 CHINESE RUNNING CLOSE CONTEST
>
> *Sub-Lieutenants Mukai and Noda in a friendly contest*

to see which of them will first fell 100 Chinese in individual sword combat ... are running almost neck to neck. On Sunday the "score" was Mukai 89, Noda 78. **(C)**

A week later the newspaper explained that the target was now 150 killings. The report went on:

Mukai's blade was slightly damaged. He explained that this was the result of cutting a Chinese in half, helmet and all. The contest was "fun" he declared. **(D)**

In December 1937 Nanjing (Nanking) fell. The Japanese committed terrible atrocities in the city, raping, murdering and torturing thousands of people.

China appealed to the League, but it had now become little more than a powerless Anglo-French club. Although Russia had joined in 1934, Germany and Italy had both left. Britain and France did nothing about China. They even continued to sell war materials to Japan. The League did condemn Japan, but agreed only on a weak proposal that each member should see what (if anything) it could do to help the Chinese. There was no longer any real attempt at collective security (see pages 14–17); that idea had died in the mid-1930s. Outside the League the USA was unwilling to take any action that might endanger its trade with Japan.

Japan ignored the League and continued to push forward. The Chinese fought as they retreated. David Bergamini, a child of 10 at the time, later recalled some of the scenes he witnessed:

I sat with my father. Through our field glasses I looked into the front lines of Japanese occupied China. Japanese soldiers were conducting a reprisal raid against a Chinese farm village, bayoneting its inhabitants and systematically burning its huts. Tomorrow there would be refugees, orphaned children, toddlers with cruel bayonet wounds ... Tomorrow night the Chinese guerillas would make a fresh sortie and bring back a few Japanese heads to mount on bamboo poles ... The Japanese soldiers took food from the starving, threw infants into the air and caught them on bayonets. **(E)**

Millions of Chinese refugees retreated west. Most had to walk, a few lucky ones found a place on a train. A nurse, Han Suyin, remembers:

... refugees huddled on the carriage roofs in the rain, or fell off in a trance of exhaustion, or were pushed off because they were dying of typhus or malaria, or simply because they tried to relieve themselves and were too weak to grip ... At every station were refugees ... a swarm moving to climb on the trains and beaten off with truncheons. **(F)**

By the end of 1938 the Japanese controlled most of eastern China (see **C** on page 34). In November 1938

Japan announced a 'New Order in East Asia'. The idea was that Japan, Manchuria and China would unite under the leadership of Japan. This was the first step towards establishing the 'Greater East Asia Co-prosperity Sphere' – a sort of common market of nearby countries under Japanese control. Japan wanted the oil, tin and rubber that these countries possessed.

The Chinese rejected the idea of the 'New Order'. The Chinese Nationalist leader Chiang Kaishek saw through the Japanese plan. In 1938 he commented:

The so-called new order is to be created after China has been reduced to a slave nation. The aim of the Japanese is to control China militarily and to eliminate Chinese culture. **(G)**

The outbreak of the Second World War in Europe in 1939 made Japan keen to extend the 'Co-prosperity Sphere'. In 1940 Japan signed the Tripartite Axis pact with Italy and Germany. Then Japanese troops invaded French Indo–China. In reply, the USA, Britain and Holland stopped the sale of oil to Japan. So Japan decided to take what it needed by force – particularly oil from Indonesia. The Japanese leaders knew this would mean war with America and Britain. They decided to strike first, by attacking the American naval base at Pearl Harbour, Hawaii, in December 1941.

??????????????

1 Explain the terms: dark valley; strike south group; Greater Co-prosperity Sphere; Tripartite Axis Pact.

2 What information does photograph **A** give about the Japanese attack on China?

3 a How far can we trust David Bergamini's description (**E**) of how the Japanese treated their enemies?
b Which other pieces of evidence (**A–F**) support it?

4 Which piece of evidence in this section do you think is:
a most trustworthy?
b least trustworthy?
Give reasons for your answer.

5 Make a list of points about the way the Japanese treated the Chinese. Then imagine it is 1937. Your school is in Nanjing. A Japanese force has surrounded the building. Say what might happen: in the next five minutes; in the next half hour; when the Japanese have left. As a survivor, write a letter to a friend telling them what happened.

6 As if you were Lieutenant Mukai (see **C** and **D**) in 1941, describe the main acts of Japanese aggression 1930–41 and explain why Japan is conquering East Asia. (Use the evidence in this and the last section to help you. Mention: Japan's problems; Manchuria/Manchukuo; Jehol; League of Nations; Britain; Greater Co-prosperity Sphere; oil; Pearl Harbour.)

18 The League of Nations: success or failure?

Do you think you are a success at school? How do you judge this? Does success depend on whether you pass your examinations? On how many friends you have? On doing as little work as possible? It all depends on your aims. To decide if something is a success we often look to see if it has achieved its aims.

The main aims of the League of Nations were:
1 to keep the peace;
2 to safeguard the independence of countries;
3 to reduce armaments;
4 to improve people's living and working conditions.

As you have seen, the League dealt successfully with several disputes in the 1920s, but in the 1930s it failed to deal effectively with the disputes over Manchuria (see chapters 16 and 17) and Abyssinia (see chapter 13).

The Abyssinian crisis was a fatal blow to the League. The historian A J P Taylor explains:

‘The real death of the League was in December 1935. One day it was a powerful body imposing sanctions; the next day it was an empty sham, everyone scuttling from it as quickly as possible.’ (A)

(*The Origins of the Second World War*, 1961)

There were further major failures for the League as German aggression led Europe into the Second World War (see chapters 19–21). It was clear that the League had failed to achieve at least the first two of its aims.

Why did the League fail? The idea of forming a league, and the actual organisation were not at fault. The problem lay with the different nations and their leaders. Many nations lacked the will to make the League work. Indeed, some wanted to make war. The British Foreign Secretary, Anthony Eden, said in 1936:

‘There was nothing wrong with the Covenant of the League. Its general principles were right. It formed a logical and reasonable system. Its shortcomings were due to the failure on the part of Members to apply the system loyally.’ (B)

The great powers put their own interests first and were not willing to take action which might damage their particular concerns, even though such action might be best for collective security. C shows other factors which contributed to the League's failure.

The League also failed in its third aim of reducing armaments. The Covenant of the League stated:

‘The maintenance of peace requires the reduction of

C Reasons for the failure of the League of Nations

Cause	Consequences
1 The USA never joined. The League was dominated by European powers – but one of the major crises was in Manchuria, a long way from Europe.	Without the USA France felt insecure and the League did not have the power in the Pacific to counter Japan's aggression.
2 Important Great Powers only belonged for brief periods (see **D**).	This reduced the League's authority. In some areas the League had little influence.
3 Members did not use the weapons available to stop aggression. They never used military sanction (joint army raised from member countries). Only used economic sanction half-heartedly.	Aggressors came to believe the League was toothless and not prepared to stand up to them.
4 Members put off making decisions, at vital moments. Meetings few and far between. Decisions made slowly – often too late.	Aggressors believed the League did not want to act.
5 The Depression meant that Governments were preoccupied by problems at home.	This helped make some countries unstable – helped Hitler come to power.
6 The League was bound to uphold terms of the Treaty of Versailles – but some terms were not satisfactory and needed to be changed.	This weakened the authority of the League. Some countries, such as Germany and Japan, which broke the terms, saw the League as an enemy.
7 Most of the responsibility for making the League work fell on Britain and France, but the governments of both countries were never strong supporters of the League. Often preferred to sign treaties outside it – eg Hoare–Laval pact.	Meant the League did not have the strong leadership it needed.

D Membership of the League – the Great Powers

	1920	1925	1930	1935	1940
Britain	————————————————————————→				
France	————————————————————————				
Japan	————————————————→ 1932 left				
Italy	————————————————————→ 1936 left				
Germany 1926 ——→ 1933 left					
Russia 1934 →1939 expelled					

Total membership 1920 = 42 nations
(17 left; 20 new members joined)

F Timechart: Attempts at disarmament

1919	Universal disarmament proposed at the Paris Peace Conference
1921	Washington Naval Conference: Britain, USA and Japan agree not to build any new battleships or cruisers for ten years and to limit the size of their fleets
1925	Locarno Treaties cause hopes for disarmament to rise
1925–30	Most countries agree disarmament is desirable but no one wants to be the first to disarm
1932	Disarmament Conference begins
1933	Germany withdraws from Conference and is already rearming
1934	Disarmament Conference ends in failure and most countries begin to rearm

H A British cartoon comment on the failure of disarmament, published in 1933

national armaments to the lowest point consistent with national safety. **(E)**

The League's job was to organise this reduction. But this was very difficult. It was not easy for countries to disarm after a long war; there was distrust between former enemies. France was particularly nervous, because it had lost the safeguard of American support when America refused to join the League. The French looked around for some other source of security. French leaders believed the best form of defence was a large army.

F outlines the main events in the League's attempts to achieve disarmament. The main effort was the Disarmament Conference of 1932–34. Germany complained that the Treaty of Versailles had forced it to disarm: other countries should now do the same. This worried the French and they obstructed plans for reducing arms. Meanwhile, Germany was secretly rearming. In 1933 the Germans withdrew from the Conference and left the League of Nations. The German Foreign Minister claimed:

‘ *The failure of the Conference was due solely to the unwillingness on the part of the highly-armed states to carry out their contractual duty to disarm.* **(G)**

Germany began to rearm openly. The idea of disarmament was dead **(H)**.

The League of Nations was a brave experiment to protect peace by collective security and reducing armaments. Although it failed in these aims, it did have some success in improving working and living conditions (the fourth aim). League agencies did much good work – providing medical help, improving international transport and radio communications, and trying to stop slavery.

???????????????

1 In your own words explain the meaning of **E**. Why was it difficult to achieve this aim?

2 Study **H**
   a What is breaking free?
   b What point is the cartoonist making about disarmament?
   c What does the reference to Professor Geneva mean?
   d In which year do you think the cartoon was drawn?

3 What are the advantages and disadvantages for the historian of the following types of sources:
   a other historians' accounts (**A**)?
   b politicians' views (**B** and **G**)?
   c cartoons (**H**)?

4 The League has been described as 'a fragile life raft on the stormy seas of the 1930s'. Explain what this means and what caused the 'raft' to sink. (Use the information on these pages and anything else you can find. Mention: aims; the Depression; disarmament; China; Abyssinia; Germany.)

19 Steps to war 1: 1934–37

The great problem in Europe during the 1920s and '30s was the strength of Germany. The Treaty of Versailles had tried to reduce and control this strength. Most Germans fiercely opposed the Treaty. In 1933 they had a new leader, Adolf Hitler, who was determined to tear up the Treaty and build up Germany's strength. The next three chapters show how, after 1935, Hitler's aggression led to the breakdown of international relations and finally to the outbreak of the Second World War (see also *Germany* in this series). The map inside the back cover of this book shows German expansion 1935–39.

As you read these chapters, think what advice *you* would have given Hitler in order to help him achieve his aims:

1 to tear up the Treaty of Versailles
2 to unite all Germans in a single country or *Reich* (empire)
3 to win *Lebensraum* (living space) for Germans in the rich farmlands of Russia and Poland.

Each time you are asked to make a *Decision* keep these aims in mind. See how many times your choices are the same as Hitler's.

Rearmament

One of the first things Hitler wanted to do was to build up the army and rearm Germany with tanks, warships and submarines. This was forbidden by the Treaty of Versailles.

Decision Which course of action should Hitler follow:
a Keep to the limits on arms set at Versailles, but try to negotiate an increase?
b Rearm secretly?
c Rearm openly?

At the Disarmament Conference in 1933–4 (see page 39) it was clear that France would not agree to any increase in Germany's armed forces. Germany had, in fact, already begun to rearm secretly. **A** is from a British Cabinet paper drawn up early in 1933.

❛It is understood that there are at least 125 fighting aircraft in existence or being made ... secret sources show that an order has been given by the German Government to the Dornier works for 36 twin-engined night bombers. The cost of these orders is to be disguised under funds for employment of the unemployed. There are numerous indications in the last two months of increased activity in the German armaments industry.❜ (**A**)

(Report by Brigadier Temperley to the Cabinet, 16 May 1933)

In 1934 Hitler began to rearm openly and withdrew Germany from the League of Nations.

Austria, the Saar and the Stresa Front

Hitler's first chance to reverse some of the terms of the Treaty of Versailles came in 1934. Under the Treaty, Germany and Austria were forbidden to unite, but in 1934 Austrian Nazis murdered the Austrian leader, Engelbert Dolfuss, and tried to take over the government. The Austrian Nazis hoped for support from Hitler. However, Mussolini wanted to protect Austria. He rushed troops to the Austrian border and warned Hitler that he would fight to stop a Nazi takeover.

Decision What should Hitler do about Austria:
a Back down and make Mussolini an ally?
b Send in troops and fight the Italians, if necessary?
c Send in troops with orders to withdraw if the Italians oppose them?

Hitler believed that Mussolini meant what he said. He was not ready for a war (course *b*), but if he followed plan *c* his control in Germany would be weakened. So Hitler chose course *a* and made an agreement with Mussolini.

Hitler's first important step towards achieving aims 2 and 3 (see above) came in 1935. Under the Treaty of Versailles a *plebiscite* (vote) was to be held in the Saar area (see map inside back cover) to allow people there to decide their future. 90% voted to become part of Germany again. This gave Hitler large new resources of coal, iron and steel.

Soon after this, Hitler openly introduced *conscription* (compulsory military service). The leaders of France, Britain and Italy were worried by Germany's growing strength. They met at Stresa in Italy to discuss what to do. The three nations formed the Stresa Front, an understanding that they would stand together against Germany. But the Stresa Front soon fell apart. First Britain upset France in 1935 by signing the Anglo-German Naval Treaty – this allowed Germany to build a navy up to 35% of the strength of the British fleet. Then, in 1936, Italy fell out with Britain and France when they opposed the Italian invasion of Abyssinia (see pages 28–29). This disagreement was crucial, because it helped push Italy into making an alliance with Germany in 1936 (the Rome–Berlin Axis) and thus helped clear the way for Germany to occupy Austria in 1938.

The Rhineland

With Britain, France and Italy quarrelling among themselves Hitler prepared his next move. The Rhineland was part of Germany, but the Treaty of Versaillies had *demilitarised* the area (no weapons or soldiers were allowed there). Hitler wanted full control of the Rhineland, but his army generals were against sending in troops. They feared that the much stronger French army would force them out.

Decision How should Hitler tackle the Rhineland:
a Take a risk by sending in troops with orders to withdraw if they meet opposition from the French army?
b Gamble and send in troops with orders to fight any opposition?
c Try to negotiate an end to demilitarisation – although the French are unlikely to agree?

On 8 March Hitler made his move. The next day, *The Times* newspaper reported:

❝German troops have marched into the demilitarised zone. The local population is naturally jubilant ... In Berlin the news appeared to be taken very calmly, even in National Socialist Party (Nazi) circles. In moderate and responsible quarters there was anxious astonishment at the decision to occupy the Rhineland ... Nevertheless, flags were hung out by the population at Dr Goebbels' request in celebration of the final re-establishment of German freedom and sovereignty ... Large crowds gathered outside the Chancery during the day and in the evening the SA (brownshirt soldiers) staged a torchlight procession with Herr Hitler taking the salute.❞ (**B**)

Hitler had chosen policy *a* – and won. He was well aware of the chance he was taking, as he later explained:

❝The 48 hours after the march into the Rhineland were the most nerve-racking in my life. If the French had then marched into the Rhineland, we would have had to withdraw with our tails between our legs, for our military resources would have been wholly inadequate for even a moderate resistance.❞ (**C**)

The march into the Rhineland was a clear breach of the Locarno Treaties and the Treaty of Versailles (**D**). So why did France and Britain make no attempt to stop it? France lacked a strong leader and had problems at home. The French would not act without British support. Britain was not willing to stop Germany. These events had important effects on Europe (see **E**).

D 'Goosey Goosey Gander, Whither dost thou wander?'
'Only through the Rhineland, Pray excuse my blunder!'
Cartoon from *Punch* magazine, March 1936 (German soldiers marched with a high-kicking step, nicknamed 'the goose step')

After 1935 Italy and Germany forged a close friendship. Hitler helped Mussolini with supplies during the invasion of Abyssinia. Then both leaders supported Franco in the Spanish Civil War. In October 1936 Hitler and Mussolini formed the Rome–Berlin Axis (**F**) in which they promised to help each other. Europe was beginning to split into two opposing sides.

E The effects of German rearmament and reoccupation of the Rhineland

1 Germany built a line of forts along the Rhine. This meant Britain and France would find it more difficult to enter Germany to stop it breaking treaties.
2 Germany could protect the great industrial area of the Ruhr.
3 France now had German troops right on its border.
4 The smaller powers saw that collective security was of little use to them, and were tempted to come to terms with Germany.
5 Hitler was encouraged to take more chances.
6 Britain and France began to rearm.

HIT AND MUSS ON THEIR AXIS

F A British cartoon on the Rome–Berlin Axis

In November 1936 Germany and Japan signed the Anti-Comintern Pact. A year later, Mussolini visited Berlin and Italy joined the Pact. Mussolini was impressed by Hitler. He told his wife:

❝ *It's unbelievable. I've never seen such a military machine with all the wheels turning so smoothly . . . We're trying to create an anti-Bolshevik front stretching across Europe.* ❞ (G)

Chart **H** outlines the steps to war 1933–37.

H The reshaping of Europe 1933–37

1933	Hitler comes to power; Germany leaves League of Nations.
1934	Mussolini prevents Anschluss of Germany and Austria.
1935	*Jan* Saar votes to return to Germany; Hitler introduces conscription.
	April Stresa Front formed – soon begins to fall apart.
	June Anglo–German Naval Treaty signed.
1936	*March* German troops reoccupy Rhineland.
	Oct Rome–Berlin Axis.
	Nov Anti-Comintern Pact between Germany and Japan.
1937	*May* Chamberlain British Prime Minister – follows policy of appeasement
	Dec Italy leaves League of Nations, joins Anti-Comintern Pact.

???????????????

1 Complete the following sentences:
  a In 1934 Mussolini prevented Hitler . . .
  b The Rome–Berlin Axis was . . .
  c In December 1937 Italy . . .

2 What evidence in **A** shows that Germany was trying to keep rearmament secret?

3 a How was the march into the Rhineland welcomed by: the people living there? people in Berlin (**B**)?
  b What does **C** tell you about Germany's military strength, 1936–7?

4 Study **D**
  a Why has the cartoonist shown a goose and referred to a 'goose step'?
  b Why is the goose trampling over a torn document?
  c Does the cartoonist support Germany's actions? Give reasons for your answer.

5 Study **F**
  a What does the cartoonist, David Low, think of the Rome–Berlin Axis?
  b David Low's cartoons were banned in Germany and Italy. Explain why you think they were banned.

6 The two cartoons, **D** and **F**, comment on events from one point of view only. Which? What other evidence might the historian wish to use to balance this view of events?

7 Which of the consequences in **E** do you think were the most important for the future of Europe? Why?

8 How did Mussolini become an ally of Hitler between 1936–7? (Mention: Austria; Stresa Front; Abyssinia; Spanish Civil War; Rome–Berlin Axis; Anti-Comintern Pact.)

20 Steps to war 2: 1937–8

Russia	Stalin's purges had weakened the Russian Army
Italy	was fully occupied with Spain, and becoming increasingly friendly with Germany
France	lacked a strong leader and would not act without British support
Britain	Neville Chamberlain became Prime Minister in May 1937. He believed in a policy of *appeasement* – which meant giving in to what he thought were reasonable demands by Germany, in the hope of avoiding war
Japan	had been Germany's ally since November 1936
USA	was following a policy of isolationism

A   The great powers in 1937

In 1937 the situation in Europe seemed to be in Hitler's favour. None of the other great powers was ready to stop Germany (see **A**). Conditions were right for Hitler to make a move towards uniting Germany and Austria (*Anschluss*). This was forbidden by the Treaty of Versailles, so Hitler tried to make it appear that Austria wanted the union. First he ordered the Austrian Nazi Party, led by Arthur Seyss-Inquart, to stir up as much trouble as possible in Austria. Then, in February 1938, Hitler invited the Austrian leader, Kurt Schuschnigg, to Germany. Much later (in 1947) Schuschnigg recalled how Hitler gave him an ultimatum:

❝I have only to give an order, and in one single night all your ridiculous defences will be blown to bits. You don't seriously believe that you can stop me for half an hour, do you? ... Don't think for one moment that anybody on earth is going to thwart my decisions. Italy? I see eye to eye with Mussolini ... England? England will not move one finger for Austria ... France? France could have stopped Germany in the Rhineland, but it is too late for France ... I give you for the last time the chance to come to terms. Think it over Herr Schuschnigg. I can only wait until this afternoon.❞ **(B)**

(Kurt Schuschnigg – written from memory in 1947)

Schuschnigg was bullied into giving Austrian Nazis important jobs in his government. The Nazis were creeping into Austria like maggots eating into a dying animal.

Schuschnigg tried to stop Hitler's plans by asking Austrians to vote on the future of their country. Hitler was furious. He knew that if the vote went against the Anschluss, he could not claim to be doing what Austrians wanted.

Decision What should Hitler do next:
a Invade Austria immediately?
b Wait and hope that the Austrians will vote for the Anschluss (this is unlikely)?
c Continue to bully Schuschnigg by moving German troops to the border and threatening to invade if he does not resign?

Hitler chose course *c*. Threatened with invasion, Schuschnigg caved in. On 12 March 1938 the Nazi leader Seyss-Inquart took control. He asked for German troops to help keep order, and proclaimed the Anschluss.

Britain and France protested but did nothing else. On 14 March 1938, Winston Churchill (who was to become Prime Minister during the war) warned the British Government:

❝Europe is confronted with a programme of aggression, there is only one choice open, not only to us but to other countries, either to submit like Austria, or else take effective measures while time remains to ward off the danger ... Where are we going to be two years hence, when the German Army will certainly be much larger than the French Army, and when all the small nations will have fled from Geneva to make up to the ever growing power of the Nazi system, and to make the best terms that they can for themselves.❞ **(C)**

Germany's position in Europe was now much stronger. Hitler had new supplies of men and materials. He was well placed to take his next step – towards the break-up of Czechoslovakia. In fact, Czechoslovakia appeared to be well protected. It had a line of fortresses along the border with Germany, and a strong, modern army. As well as receiving protection under the Treaty of Versailles, Czechoslovakia had made alliances with France, Russia, Rumania and Yugoslavia.

Yet despite all this, it took Hitler less than a year to take control over most of Czechoslovakia and break up the rest. How did he do it? Points in Hitler's favour were the *appeasement* policies (attempts to make terms rather than go to war) of Britain and France, and the presence of three million German-speaking Sudetens living in the Sudetenland area of Czechoslovakia (see map inside back cover). The Sudetenland was stuck like a fish in the jaws of a shark – and Hitler began to close the jaws.

Decision How would you advise Hitler to go about the destruction of Czechoslovakia (March–September 1938)? Should he:

a Invade immediately and hope Czechoslovakia's allies will not help?

b Order Henlein, leader of the Nazi-style Sudeten German Party, to stir up trouble in the Sudetenland? Then he could claim that the Czechs were mistreating the Sudeten, and threaten to use force to protect them.

c Not use force but try to negotiate to make the Sudetenland part of Germany?

The Czech defences were too strong to chance invasion (course *a*) and the Czechs, led by President Eduard Benes, would never willingly agree to hand over the Sudetenland (course *c*). So Hitler chose course *b*. Henlein organised riots and demonstrations and the Sudetens clashed with the Czech police. On 26 September 1938 Hitler spoke to the German people, to prepare them:

❝*The territory which belongs to Germans and which Germany wants shall become German, and not after Benes has succeeded in exterminating one or two million Germans, but now – immediately ... It is the last territorial claim which I have to make in Europe ... There*

E How Chamberlain tried to avoid war, August–September 1938

Prague (*August*) Lord Runciman led a British mission to help the Sudetens and Czechs reach an agreement – this failed.

Berchtesgaden (*15 Sept*) Hitler insisted Sudetenland became part of Germany but promised Chamberlain time to talk to France. Britain and France forced Czechs to agree to Hitler's demands by saying they would not help if Czechoslovakia was attacked.

Godesberg (*22 Sept*) Hitler now said Germany must march into Sudetenland immediately. Britain and France did not agree – began to prepare for war.

Munich (*29 Sept*) At the last moment Hitler agreed to a four-power conference (Britain, France, Germany, Italy) at Munich. (Neither Czechoslovakia nor Russia invited). Hitler, Mussolini, Chamberlain and Daladier of France agreed:
1 German troops to occupy Sudetenland;
2 Claims of Poland and Hungary on Czechoslovakian territory should be met;
3 Britain and France would protect what was left of Czechoslovakia.

G The Munich Conference, 1938. British Prime Minister Neville Chamberlain is on the left of the picture; Hitler in the centre; Mussolini second from the right

is no such thing as a Czechoslovak nation, but only Czechs and Slovaks, and the Slovaks do not wish to have anything to do with the Czechs . . . villages (in the Sudetenland) are burned down, attempts are made to smoke out the Germans with hand-grenades and gas . . . my patience is now at an end. The decision now lies in Benes' hands: Peace or War. He will either accept our offer and now at last give the Sudeten Germans their freedom, or we will go and fetch this freedom. (**D**)

Britain and France were worried. France had promised to help protect Czechoslovakia in a treaty signed in 1934. So an attack by Germany could easily lead to another major war. From August–September 1938, Britain and France tried hard to avoid war, pressing Czechoslovakia to accept each new demand made by Hitler. Finally, in September, the British Prime Minister, Neville Chamberlain, flew to Germany three times to meet Hitler and try to find a solution (**E**). Afterwards, Chamberlain said of Hitler:

'In spite of the hardness and ruthlessness I thought I saw in his face, I got the impression that here was a man who could be relied upon when he had given his word.' (**F**)

At a final meeting in Munich (**G**), Britain and France deserted Czechoslovakia and gave in to Hitler's demands for the Sudetenland. Czechoslovakia either had to accept the Munich Agreement or fight Germany – and probably Poland and Hungary as well. The Czechs agreed, and on 1 October 1938 German troops marched into the Sudetenland. **H** shows how people in Britain felt about Hitler's actions.

H Results of public opinion polls in Britain

		Result
March 1938 *Should Britain promise assistance to Czechoslovakia if Germany acts as it did towards Austria?*	Yes	33%
	No	43%
	No opinion	24%
October 1938 *Hitler says he has 'No more territorial ambitions in Europe'. Do you believe him?*	Yes	7%
	No	93%
February 1939 *Which of these statements comes nearest to representing your view of Mr Chamberlain's policy of appeasement:*		
1 *It is a policy which will ultimately lead to a lasting peace in Europe*		28%
2 *It will keep us out of war until we have time to rearm*		46%
3 *It is bringing war nearer by whetting the appetites of the dictators*		24%
No opinion		2%
April 1939 *Is the British Government right in following a policy of giving guarantees to preserve the independence of small European nations?*	Yes	83%
	No	17%

??????????????????

1 a Why might a historian doubt the accuracy of Schuschnigg's account (**B**)?

b How does Hitler justify trying to break up Czechoslovakia in **D**?

c What did Churchill mean in **C** when he said 'all the small nations will have fled from Geneva'?

d How far do sources **B**, **C** and **D** help us to explain Hitler's aims? What other evidence would a historian want to consult?

2 a Which two sources in this section directly contradict each other about Hitler's aims? How?

b Is there any other primary evidence on these pages which supports either view?

3 Study **H**

a In March 1938, did the majority of the public questioned support the policy which Chamberlain followed six months later at Munich?

b What does the poll suggest about the public's view of appeasement in February 1939?

c How did British opinion about appeasement change between March 1938 and April 1939?

d Imagine you are a journalist interviewing someone who has answered 'Yes' in the October 1938 opinion poll. You ask her how she feels about the threat from Germany and the possibility of war. Write out the interview. Which statement in the February 1939 poll would such a person be likely to choose?

4 Mussolini said 'Czechoslovakia was not just Czechoslovakia but Czecho-Germano-Polono-Magyaro-Rutheno-Roumano-Slovakia'. Explain what he meant and how this helped Hitler to destroy Czechoslovakia.

21 Steps to war 3: Poland

Chamberlain arrived home from Munich on 30 September 1938 claiming he brought peace with Germany. He waved a piece of paper which he and Hitler had signed. It said:

We regard the Munich Agreement as a sign of the desire of our two people never to go to war with one another again. (A)

Most British people welcomed Chamberlain as a hero. They believed he had averted the threat of war, and they supported the policy of appeasement. **B** shows the real results of appeasing Hitler at Munich.

B The consequences of appeasement at Munich

1 Hitler gained Czechoslovakia – including the great Skoda arms factory.
2 Hitler was encouraged into thinking Britain and France would not act to protect other countries, eg Poland.
3 Germany was not ready in September 1938 to fight Czechoslovakia, Britain and France. The agreement gave time to prepare for war. Germany used this time much better than Britain and France.
4 Britain and France at last learned Hitler would not keep any agreement.
5 France's allies – Poland, Yugoslavia and Rumania – lost confidence in France and tried to improve relations with Germany.
6 Russia, which had been prepared to help Czechoslovakia, believed Britain and France could not be relied on.

Not everyone supported appeasement; Winston Churchill warned:

We have suffered a total defeat. I think you will find that in a period of time Czechoslovakia will be engulfed by the Nazis ... all the countries of Central and Eastern Europe will make the best terms they can with the triumphant Nazi power. The system of alliances upon which France has relied for her safety has been swept away ... And do not suppose that this is the end. This is only the beginning of the reckoning. (C)

Churchill was right. The end of Czechoslovakia quickly followed on from the Munich Agreement. **D** shows the steps to war March 1938–September 1939. It was now clear that Hitler intended to do more than simply unite the German-speaking peoples. The smaller nations in Europe were worried. The *New York Times* newspaper reported:

1938 *Mar* Anschluss of Germany and Austria
Sept Chamberlain visits Hitler: Munich Agreement
Oct German troops occupy the Sudetenland; Poland seizes Teschen (to March 1939)
1939 *Mar* Hungary seizes southern Czechoslovakia and Ruthenia. Slovakia declares independence. German troops invade Bohemia and Moravia. Hitler forces Lithuania to hand over Memel.
May Italy seizes Albania. Britain and France guarantee to help Greece and Rumania if attacked. Germany and Italy sign Pact of Steel.
Aug Germany and Russia sign Non-Aggression Pact (Molotov–Ribbentrop Pact)
1 Sept German troops invade Poland.
3 Sept Britain and France declare war on Germany.

D The reshaping of Europe, March 1938–Sept 1939

Every nation in Europe is doing what it can to shove Germany away from its own frontier in the direction of the other fellow. The Foreign Ministers of Yugoslavia, Hungary and Poland will move heaven and earth to prevent Germany driving East – not of course by thinking to fight Germany but by encouraging Germany to go West. (E)

Hitler had his eye on Poland. The Treaty of Versailles had split East Prussia off from the rest of Germany by giving land to Poland – creating a Polish 'corridor' to the sea. At the end of the corridor was the international city of Danzig. Most of the people in Danzig were German. Hitler wanted both the city and the corridor.

Britain and France realised that appeasement was not working. Public opinion was no longer in favour of keeping on good terms with Germany. Britain and France promised to support Poland if it was attacked. Hitler thought they were bluffing. Poland refused to give in to Hitler's bullying. A Polish newspaper declared:

The whole people will fight with determination for Polish freedom and independence. Nothing will be given up without a fight. Every Polish house will be a fortress which the enemy will have to take by storm. The danger from the air will not daunt Poland ... Whoever seeks a quarrel with Poland will have more to lose than to gain. (F)

Britain and France tried (although not very hard) to reach agreement with Russia for help against Germany. But Stalin, the Russian leader, was suspicious of them.

تقدم التعاون الألماني الروسي

H The Nazi–Soviet Pact

In May, Hitler warned his officers:

❝ *. . . There is no question of sparing Poland and we are left with the decision: to attack Poland at the first suitable opportunity. We cannot expect a repetition of the Czech affair. There will be a war. Our task is to isolate Poland.* ❞ (**G**)

Hitler knew that Stalin, the Russian leader, was suspicious of Britain and France. He wanted to take advantage of this distrust, so he chose policy *b*. On 23 August Germany and Russia signed a Non-Aggression Pact (**H**). This agreement amazed the world. Stalin later explained, in a radio broadcast on 3 July 1941:

❝ *We secured peace for our country for one and a half years, as well as an opportunity of preparing our forces for defence if fascist Germany risked attacking our country in defiance of the pact. This was a definite gain for Russia and a loss for fascist Germany.* ❞ (**J**)

Stalin did not feel Russia could rely on Britain and France, who had already deserted Czechoslovakia. Also, the Munich Agreement encouraged Germany to expand eastwards. He needed to buy time for Russia to prepare for war, and he hoped that Germany would be weakened by fighting Britain and France first.

Hitler thought the pact with Russia would make it even less likely that Britain and France would help Poland. On 1 September 1939 German troops invaded Poland. Mussolini suggested a conference, but Britain and France did not want to repeat what had happened at Munich. On 3 September they declared war on Germany. The Second World War had begun.

Hitler had all this in mind as he prepared to attack Poland. He knew the German army was ready to invade Poland, but not strong enough to tackle any other country. If he did attack, Russia would feel threatened, and might help Poland. Most of all, Hitler wanted to avoid having to fight Britain and France in the West at the same time as fighting Russia in the East. This had happened in the First World War, and had been a major factor in the defeat of Germany.

Decision What policy should Hitler follow in September 1939 to avoid having to fight Britain and France at the same time as fighting Russia:

a Attack Poland and hope Britain and France will back down as before?

b Agree with Russia not to attack each other and to divide up Poland between you, then attack Poland?

c Attack France and Britain as well as Poland, even though your army is not yet ready and Russia might join with your enemies?

??????????????

1 a Which do you think were the two most important results of appeasement (**B**)? Give reasons for your answer.

b Does **E** support or contradict Churchill's views in **C**?

c What do **F** and **G** agree about?

2 Study **H**

a How does the cartoonist show Stalin and Hitler had made an agreement or pact?

b What do you think the cartoonist felt about the agreement? Give reasons for your answer.

3 a Which of the following people do you think would be most likely to follow a policy of appeasement: a coward; someone who desperately wants to avoid the horror of war; someone wanting to buy time to prepare for a fight; a fool; someone who misjudges other people?

b Which of these do you think applies to Chamberlain? What evidence from the last two chapters supports your choice?

22 Conclusion

September 1939. The map of Europe (see opposite) looked very different from that drawn up in the peace treaties of 1919. Germany had recovered its strength. Czechoslovakia had been taken over. Austria was no longer independent. Poland would be divided between Germany and Russia before the end of the month. Most of the safeguards against war set up by the peace treaties had been swept away.

Fascism had replaced democracy in the governments of Germany and Italy. Fascist-style dictators controlled Spain and Portugal. The USSR was firmly in the grip of the communist dictator, Stalin. The great hopes for collective security promised by the League of Nations had long since died. Insecurity, fear and aggression had led countries to form alliances with friends and enemies alike, and build up their armaments.

Since the mid-1930s the threat of war had been growing – brought nearer by the Italian invasion of Abyssinia, the Spanish civil war and, finally, the destruction of Czechoslovakia. Ed Murrow, an American broadcaster in London, recognised these important turning points. Just before Britain and France declared war, he reported to Americans:

❛I have a feeling that Englishmen are a little proud of themselves tonight: they believe the Lion has turned and that the retreat from Manchukuo, Abyssinia, Spain, Austria and Czechoslovakia has stopped.❜ (A)

Soon, millions of refugees would be walking the roads of Europe (B).

Meanwhile, Japan had become a leading world power. The USA was once again beginning to be concerned with Europe's political affairs, turning away from the policy of isolationism. Many Americans were worried by Japanese expansion in the Far East and the rise of fascism in Europe. Between 1939 and 1941, America took steps to forge a closer friendship with Britain (C).

The last of these steps, the Atlantic Charter, meant isolationism was dead. It was buried when Japan attacked the American base at Pearl Harbour in December 1941.

C How America was drawn into war

1939	*Neutrality Act* – allowed the sale of weapons to Britain
1941	America banned the sale of chemicals, scrap iron and oil to Japan
	Lend–Lease Act – America lent supplies to Britain, although it could not afford to pay for them
	Atlantic Charter – America and Britain declared a series of joint aims for Europe after the war

B Belgian refugees fleeing from the German advance